GRILLED
TO PERFECTION

CHRIS KNIGHT & TYLER J. SMITH

RECIPES FROM THE TELEVISION SERIES
LICENCE TO GRILL

McArthur & Company
Toronto

First published in Canada in 2006 by
McArthur & Company
322 King St. West, Suite 402
Toronto, Ontario
M5V 1J2
www.mcarthur-co.com

Copyright © 2006 Chris Knight

Library and Archives Canada Cataloguing in Publication

Knight, Chris, 1960-
Grilled to perfection : recipes from licence to grill / Chris Knight.

ISBN 1-55278-568-8

1. Barbecue cookery. I. Title.

TX840.B3K55 2006   641.7'6   C2006-901923-1

Design by *Mad Dog Design Inc.*
Front cover author photo by *Denise Grant*
Printed in Canada by *Transcontinental*

The publisher would like to acknowledge the financial support of the Government of Canada through the Book Publishing Industry Development Program, the Canada Council for the Arts, and the Ontario Arts Council for our publishing activities. We also acknowledge the Government of Ontario through the Ontario Media Development Corporation Ontario Book Initiative.

10 9 8 7 6 5 4 3 2

*To my son Adam,
to my mother Carolle*

Contents

Preface

Welcome to the *License To Grill* cookbook. By the time you read this, we will have finished 104 episodes of the television series. That's a pretty staggering number of shows, and *License To Grill* has resonated with viewers the world over since it first went to air not so long ago. Making a television show takes a lot of hard work from a lot of very creative people. Making a great show like *License To Grill* (if I do say so myself) requires the perfect alignment of the proverbial planets. First you need a great idea. In this case, it's a backyard barbecue show where every episode takes place on a Saturday afternoon with friends coming over for dinner that night. Then you need a savvy broadcaster. We have Food Network Canada who in turn have Karen Gelbart, Eleanor James and Tom Hastings who gave us the nod and then helped keep us pointed in the right direction with guidance, input and advice. Then you need to get a host . . . a great host. We found just the guy in Rob Rainford. From scene 1, Episode 1 we knew that Rob was going to be a hit. His easygoing style, natural charm and enthusiasm for all things barbecue has made Rob a huge hit and a welcome friend in millions of viewer's homes.

Most of all, you need amazing people working behind the scenes. Senior Producer Kathy Doherty and Director Matt West are as much responsible for the look and feel of this show as anyone. Then you've got a killer crew of camerapersons, audio, production assistants, grip, lighting, shoppers, drivers . . . the whole bunch chosen from the best in the business came together and just flowed. There was a buzz and rhythm to this bunch.

And then there's the food. Everything you see on *License To Grill* was cooked behind the scenes by Kerry Galvin. Kerry is a Force Of Nature, full of passion and creativity and an insane work ethic to boot. All the recipes on the show were developed by me along with Kerry and Kathy—it's them you have to thank for all

the good eats. The debt of gratitude I owe to everyone who has contributed to the success of the *License To Grill* experience would stun a team of oxen!

As for this book, most of the heavy lifting was done by Tyler J. Smith.
Thank you Tyler.

And finally, there's you: the viewer, the reader, the *bbqiste*. There are lots of cookbooks out there you could have picked and lots of food shows to watch. Thank you for using ours. Hope you like what we've done here.

Drop us a line at **info@knight-tv.com** and let us know.

Chris Knight

CHAPTER ONE

Size Matters After All

Big is not necessarily better when it comes to the size of your grill. When making this potentially expensive purchase, keep in mind the number of people you will be feeding. If you've got ten kids and two sets of grandparents to feed, go for something roomy. However, if you routinely feed a family of four, going smaller is a good idea. It's cheaper to heat and less work to maintain.

Just like every piece of equipment we buy, the barbecue industry has a set of standards, and no, thankfully, a PhD in physics is not required to figure it out. Simply put, the size of a barbecue is measured in terms of "total square inches." How do they come up with that total? Well, here is the "magic" formula:

Primary Square Inches: Is the total number of inches on the main cooking surface. For practical purposes, this is the most important measurement.

Secondary Square Inches: Refers to the size of the warming racks located above the main grilling racks. Not all barbecues come with this feature.

Total Square Inches: Refers to the total square inches of the two rack surfaces combined.

Which Size Do You Need?

Industry standard allocates 50-60 square inches of primary cooking surface for each portion of food cooked. I know that may sound like a lot, but remember you'll need some room to maneuver the food on the cooking surface. For us less technical folks who don't want to take a measuring tape to the barbecue store, the size of your hand is about one portion of food. Two hands will represent a meal consisting of meat and veggies. Think about the largest number of people that you will routinely cook for and aim for that size. Remember though, you want to keep your options open to avoid frustrating cooking experiences.

Can't Stand The Heat?

BTU Who? What? The dreaded BTU, every good barbecue salesperson will be able to tell you that BTU stands for British Thermal Unit. "What is that?" you might ask. (But if you really don't care, skip this part.) A BTU is a scientific measurement of how much energy is expended to raise one pound of water one degree Fahrenheit. What's that got to do "with the price of chicken?!" When referring to barbecues, BTU is the measurement of the maximum output of heat that the barbecue produces with all burners on high.

A consensus among barbecue companies suggest that between 110 to 125 BTUs per square inch is ideal for year-round cooking. This will allow you to pre-heat your barbecue quickly to between 500-600 degrees Fahrenheit within 6 to 9 minutes on an average summer day. Note, a good barbecue with accurate control valves should allow you to lower the temperature for consistent cooking temperature. Be careful with barbecues with a BTU rating of above 125 BTUs per square inch. If the control valves are not of high quality, the temperature will be harder to lower and regulate, thus producing "burnt offerings." If you live in a colder climate and wish to barbecue year round, you'll want a barbecue with a higher BTU rating per square inch to regulate cooking temperatures.

CHAPTER TWO

Gas It Up

Taste Over Convenience?

Myth or fact? You can't get an authentic barbecue flavor from a gas grill. Question: Is charcoal cooking really that cumbersome?

Charcoal Grilling — Only for the Adventurous?

For a nice outer crust on a cut of meat, charcoal grilling is certainly more effective. Very few gas barbecues can reach the level of heat that a charcoal-lit fire can. And for long, slow cooking, tradition has proven that charcoal grilling produces a wonderfully tender, smoke-infused flavor that we all strive for. So if charcoal is so wonderful, then why bother cooking with gas? Well, if you've got 30 minutes to whip up a dinner before soccer practice and you just happen to want to put a chicken breast on your charcoal grill, it's going to take you longer to light the charcoal than it will to cook the chicken!

Come On Baby Light Your Fire

In the "old days" of grilling, people would arrange the charcoal bricks in a pile, douse it with lighter fluid and everyone would "ooh" and "ahh" as the match was struck, the flames shot up to the sky and the roof burnt down. Seriously – the bigger the flame, not necessarily the better the fire and certainly not the better the food! Too much lighter fluid makes the food taste like, well, lighter fluid. We now have the option of self-lighting bricks, with the starter infused in the charcoal.

To avoid using chemicals, try using a flue starter or chimney starter. You can buy these cylindrical-shaped metal chimneys or just make one, by cutting the top and bottom off a large 39-oz can. Using the triangle end of your can opener, punch six holes along the bottom of the can for air vents. Bear in mind, for larger barbecues you will need a starter that is at about 7 inches across and at least 11 inches tall to ensure that it holds enough bricks to spread over the bottom of your grill, thus avoiding having to add cold bricks later, adding to your pre-heating time. Your barbecue salesperson can show you different varieties, sizes and prices to suit your needs. Place the flue starter on the charcoal grate (not the cooking grate). Layer with a fast-igniting dry material, like newspaper. Next, add your charcoal and/or woodchips and light from the bottom. After approximately15–20 minutes — when the coals are burning to a consistent orangey red color with a thin gray layer of ash on them — remove the cylinder and spread the coals across the bottom of your barbecue.

Probably easiest of all however, is an electric starter. In its basic form, an electric starter is a small exposed element, usually in a ring shape, with a handle. Place the element among the coals, turn it on and wait about 15 minutes. Carefully remove and place on a non-flammable surface to cool before storing away. Voila! Easy; no mess, no hassle, just a bit of time and electricity.

Regardless of the method you use to start your charcoal fire, make sure that there is a fine layer of gray ash on the bricks before you start to cook. The gray ash is a signal that the bricks are hot enough to remain fairly consistent in temperature. Also, don't scrimp on the amount of charcoal you use. More charcoal can mean a longer pre-heat time, but there should be enough to fully cover the bottom of your grill. And don't forget to pre-heat your grilling surface as well. Once the coals are hot and you've spread them out, place the grill on top to heat up – for about 5 minutes. And lastly, don't use the cover for grilling. The off-gassing from the build up of old fumes on the inside of the cover can infuse your food with a bitter chemical taste. If you want to cover or tent your food while cooking, use tinfoil or an aluminum plate.

Take Your Temperature

Because there are no handy-dandy little temperature knobs on a charcoal barbecue to manipulate the temperature of your grill, you'll need to move the hot coals around to create your different temperature zones.

A single layer of charcoal will produce direct heat that is moderate in temperature. This is good for foods that require little cooking time, like a thin fillet of fish, cut veggies or hamburgers. Single layers are also good for longer cooking, called slow roasting.

Two layers of charcoal will bring the coals closer to the food and concentrates more heat in the area that is doubled. This is great for searing meat. Being creative with the layers allows you to have both high and moderate heating surfaces at one time. For instance, for food that needs to cook slowly, thin out the coals from that area of the barbecue. For foods that need to sear, bank the coals at that end of the barbecue, thus producing multiple zones for cooking.

Your barbecue will have side vents along the bottom half. To add more oxygen to the coals, making them hotter, open the vents wider. To cool down the bricks, close the vents accordingly. Be careful though. If you have the lid down and all the vents are closed your fire will die, along with your hopes for a great meal.

To take the temperature of your grill you could buy a cooking thermometer. Or, for us hardy types, judge high heat (roughly 400F), by placing your hand about 4 inches above the grill and counting how many seconds your hand can remain there before you must move it. Should be about 2 seconds. For medium to high heat (375F), about 3 seconds. For medium heat (350F), about 5 seconds and for low heat (250F), about 7 seconds.

Gas It Up

For those of us who want to get the job done quickly and easily, with little mess and preparation, barbecuing with gas is the way to go. You turn a few knobs, ignite, wait 10 minutes and you're cooking with fire. No muss, no fuss.

Even though most gas barbecues don't get as hot as charcoal grills, you can control the temperatures of your cooking surface easier and more accurately than you can with charcoal. No moving coals around and opening and closing vents. And you can cook with the lid down, as there are no noxious fumes from lighter fluid build up on the lid to contaminate your food. This makes searing more efficient and creates even temperatures for long slow roasting. For these reasons, the majority of recipes in this book have instructions for cooking on a gas barbecue.

Want a Light?

When lighting a gas grill, follow the manufacturer's directions. Industry standards require that you light the grill with the lid open. Once lit, close the lid. Leave all burners on high until your desired temperature is reached, then lower accordingly. If your barbecue's automatic igniter is not functional, use a match or barbecue lighter and insert it into the hole in the side of the grill that is provided by the manufacturer for this very purpose. Follow the directions as above.

What's Your Number?

How many burners do you need? In order to cook using indirect heat (for roasting and smoking), you will need a minimum of two burners – one burner that is lit and one burner that is either off or on a low setting. Any more than two depends on how much food you typically cook at one time and how many different temperature zones you might need.

Running Out Of Gas?

Okay, you've got your mother-in-law coming over and five kids jumping up and down for your attention. You've just spent fifty bucks on steaks and you've got that look of determination that comes from needing a good red meat fix. You've got the grill going, the steaks have started searing then suddenly – the flame dies. You've run out of gas! Ways to prevent this:

1) Have a gas line run to the barbecue – you'll NEVER run out!

2) Buy a tank with a gas level gauge on it and always have an extra tank that is full and ready to go. Store extra tanks in a dry, cool environment.

3) If you already have a perfectly usable tank, you can check the gas level by pouring a cup of boiling water down the side of the tank, and then running your

hand along it. Where the tank is empty it will feel warm to the touch. Where the tank is full, it will feel cooler to the touch.

If you've done all that, you have enough gas and your barbecue still won't light, did you remember to turn on the gas tank? If all else fails, check to make sure you're not dealing with a clogged or bent hose that needs to be attended to.

CHAPTER THREE

All Washed Up

When most of us get our barbecues home we discard the maintenance manual faster than yesterday's newspaper. However, maintenance and regular cleaning is of vital importance to the longevity of your grill, affecting not only its performance and safety, but the taste and nutritional value of your food as well.

Rub A Dub Dub

For charcoal grills, it is important to keep the bottom of your grill free of ashes, charcoal bits and grease. This will ensure that the vents at the bottom of the barbecue are clear, providing the coals with the necessary oxygen to keep them lit and hot. Make sure ashes are cool to the touch before disposing of them.

Also, grease build-up on your grill makes it susceptible to grease fire flare-ups and leaves a chemical or acidic taste on your food. For all types of barbecues, remove the racks and wash out the interiors and the grill with warm soapy water. A light scouring pad is fine to use, but must be avoided on painted and stainless steel surfaces, as it will scratch the finish. Check your manufacturer's instructions (which you have kept in a safe place), if warm soapy water is not getting the job done.

Everyone has a different way to clean the grilling racks, from *don't clean them at all because it will remove the flavor* (not great advice!), to *place grills between thicknesses of newspaper, cover with soapy water, let soak all day, then scour and rinse*. The best advice is to clean as you cook. After your grill is lit, and before you start cooking, give your racks a quick scour with a long-handled metal brush, then coat with oil or cooking spray. After your food is cooked and removed from the grill, turn all elements to high heat again. Once heated, turn off the elements and scour the racks with a wire brush. A wide, industrial-strength sponge soaked with water will also work, as it will help steam-clean the racks. Rub clean racks dry and coat with cooking oil. This will aid in preventing rusting. These simple steps, which take up so little time, will prolong the life of your grilling racks, prevent noxious grease build-up and save you from using up too much "elbow grease."

If you're using a gas barbecue, the drip pan under the grill should be cleaned out regularly to avoid ignition. Remove lava rocks from the bottom of the grill, take out any that are broken and covered in grease and replace. Check your burners to make sure the flames emanating from them are consistent and that each has a blue-tipped flame. Clear a clogged burner with an untwisted paper clip, with the barbecue off and cool. Check all connector hoses for bugs and spiders, especially after a period of sitting unused.

Before storing for the winter, after the barbecue is completely cleaned, turn elements on high for 10 minutes to dry out all parts. Oil the racks and store covered in a dry room. Disconnect the gas tank and store it in a well-ventilated area.

CHAPTER FOUR

Tools of the Trade

If you can't stand the heat, get longer oven mitts, tongs and spatulas. Reaching into a hot oven can give you a burn you can do without. It's important to learn which utensils make sense for cooking over an open fire.

Brush Your Grill

We've discussed at length the importance of keeping your grilling racks clean. But which brush cleans the best? A brush with a sturdy, durable and LONG handle of at least 12 inches that feels comfortable in your hand is a must. While there are many kinds of grill brushes with various handles available now, the most durable handle is still one made of wood; quite often "poplar" as a matter of fact. Aluminum and various other metal handles look sturdy and attractive, however they conduct heat very quickly thus making the user wear an oven mitt, which quite frankly makes the whole procedure a slippery affair.

I would recommend two types of brushes for your grill. The first is a brush with brass bristles and are available at most hardware and department stores. The next is a new one on the market that has stainless steel pads instead of bristles. These pads are washable and replaceable and do an excellent job.

Tongs Of Choice

Most of us at one time have purchased the barbecue utensil sets that contained a giant fork. That two-pronged fork is usually the first thing people will use to turn over their hard-earned masterpieces on the grill because it is familiar to our everyday lives. And while the giant fork is indeed very useful for carving meat, be careful. All that time spent searing in juices will be for naught if you're going to go around piercing your food while it is still cooking.

Tongs are the answer. At first tongs can feel a bit awkward to use, but get a strong spring-loaded pair and you'll be purchasing one for the kitchen as well. You'll need a pair that is delicate enough at the ends to grasp fine foods like asparagus. Watch out for serrated edges though; they are often too sharp and can nick the food. Look for tongs with scalloped edges, the surface of which are perfect for just about anything you'll need to maneuver on the grill. Make sure the handle is long enough. Up to 16 inches will allow you to reach to the back of most grills without having to climb in it yourself. A longer handle also needs to be built to last, as it will bend under the weight of a roasted whole chicken for instance. Also, make sure the pincers will spread wide enough to get around something like a drumstick or a small roast.

Spatula Anyone?

Next to your tongs, your spatula will be a workhorse for you. Again, look for something with a long, sturdy handle. I like to use a spatula that is called a "dogleg" or "offset" spatula. That refers to the angle of the blade as compared to the handle. Look for one that has a large lifting surface that will be equally good for lifting a burger as it will a piece of salmon – approximately 3 inches wide by 6 inches long will lift just about everything you need it to. The blade should be thin enough in the front to get under something delicate like a piece of fish, but sturdy enough to ensure that it won't break if you have to scrape something stuck on the grill.

Brushes and A Mop

Not all marinating brushes are created equal and by far the best are the natural boar's hair brushes. Don't be fooled by the nylon varieties. You can almost always detect them because the bristles tend to be transparent and the price is usually cheaper. The boar's hair brush works well, because it stands up to the heat, absorbs liquids at a high rate, doesn't fray and washes well in hot water. The nylon bristles, on the other hand, tend to clump and are not nearly as absorbent as the natural variety. While I do like the feel of a wooden handle, they don't hold up in the dishwasher very well. Look for a brush with a thick plastic handle. You can put it in the dishwasher, making cleaning clingy marinade easier. Choose shorter handled brushes for in the kitchen and smaller jobs on the grill, longer handles for larger cuts of meat and larger quantities of food.

Before purchasing your brush, have a look at the "collar" that attaches the bristles to the handle. You want this collar to be extremely tight. There should be no wiggle room. This will help to avoid getting marinade up into the joint, making it easier to clean and will ensure you lose fewer bristles with use over time.

Also nice, particularly if you're cooking for an audience, is to take a bunch of herbs, such as rosemary, tie it into a bouquet and use that as a brush. Now, don't count on that imparting a whole lot of the flavor on your food, it will a bit, but mainly it looks esthetically pleasing and it's kind of nice for a change. You'll look like you really know what you're doing!

Relatively new to the market are silicone brushes. They don't burn, can be taken apart and put in the dishwasher. Although they aren't absorbent they are still a great option, and the price points are very reasonable in all sizes as they are extremely durable!

Last but certainly by no means least is a "brush" called "The Sauce Mop" or "The Mop" as I call it. This product looks exactly like it sounds, like a floor mop. Not a fancy new one that can power a jet engine by itself, but one of those old fashion kinds that your Grandma used to have in the closet by the back door off the kitchen. Not too appetizing you say? You might change your mind when you taste the results of this marinating tool. It's perfect for a rack of ribs or other big jobs. Made of 100% cotton, it sops up the sop and makes short work of flavoring your short ribs.

Mister

You've spent all that time preparing your prize-winning marinade, diligently brushing it over your butcher's cut of meat with your favorite boar's hair brush, then tragedy strikes. You have a flare up on your grill that is threatening your meal! Quick! Grab a plant mister and spray that fire down. Keep it close at hand and you can't go wrong.

Oil That Grill Grid

Grill pan, grill wok, grill skillet; notice a pattern here? Never has there been an easier time to cook just about anything you can imagine over an open fire. You can pan-fry, stir-fry and grill veggies without the risk of them falling into the fire, now that there is literally some sort of barbecue basket or contraption available for almost everything. The grill grid I've been using is made with a Teflon coating, which keeps the food from sticking to it.

Illicit Kitchen Syringe?

No, you will not get arrested for this injection. If you have a cut of meat that you think might need a bit more flavoring, or you need to preserve moisture during a long roast, you might want to get out the syringe. A syringe in the kitchen you might ask? Dip the syringe in your marinade, pierce the skin to the center and inject! Do this periodically while cooking, making sure to leave enough cooking time at the end to bring the injected marinade up to the appropriate temperature.

Where's The Heat?

My favorite thermometer has a sensor that you sink into the raw meat before you put it on the grill. If you are using a charcoal grill, you snake the wire that attaches to the digital sensor through the vent at the top. If you're using a gas barbecue, simply pull it through to one side of the lid. The sensor sits outside your grill and will tell you when your meat has reached the desired cooking temperature.

Skewed Up

There aren't a whole lot of choices in the marketplace as of yet of viable materials for barbecue skewers. You'll find stainless steel, bamboo or wood (and various combinations of all three). I personally prefer wood or bamboo, but then again, I'm a hands-on kind of cook. I like the organic feel of it, the look of it and they aren't as hot to handle as metal right off the grill. Stainless steel is also a fine choice. As with wood, you have to watch for food sticking to the skewers, but unlike wood, they stay hot for a long time, so care is needed off the grill. They can be pricey if you're serving kebabs to the whole neighborhood and the basketball team thus requiring more than just a few. However that said, they are reusable, where wood is definitely not.

Now obviously the down side with the wood is that it's wood. And wood does tend to burn when over a flame! People will tell you if you soak them they won't catch on fire. Well, that's not exactly true. The truth is, if you soak them they won't catch on fire *as quickly*. I soak mine for about 2 hours. Then I put tin foil under the bare handles on the barbecue to lessen the exposure to direct heat.

Something that is kind of cool is a double skewer. It's shaped like a "U," so you can thread two skewers at a time. This is advantageous because they won't rotate around on themselves making turning them over on the grill easier and allows for more even cooking.

Bag It

Want to know the secret of how to get a perfectly marinated anything, without a whole lot of muss and fuss? Use a sealable plastic bag! It's an "all in one kitchen aid." I pour the ingredients for my rubs and marinades directly in the bag. Then, I add my washed and trimmed meats and throw it in the fridge, freezer or whatever suits at the time. When needed, I take the meat out of the bag and put it directly on the grill – easy – and no mess.

Light The Way

Nothing spoils a romantic night cooking under the stars like serving burnt offerings to your guests. It's necessary to be able to see the grill, and I've found for such occasions a barbecue grill light fits the bill and keeps the party going. These durable all-weather lights mount directly onto your barbecue's handle. The lamp head can pivot for direct-task lighting when needed, but is also strong enough to illuminate the whole grill. They usually run on batteries and the good ones have an automatic shut off mechanism so the batteries are not wasted.

CHAPTER FIVE

History Anyone?

Those of you interested in a little history are in for a treat. Since no one knows for sure exactly where the word "barbecue" came from, there's a theory for everyone. Some experts have said the word may have come from Native American Indians who called their practice of roasting meat over coals "barbacoa." The settlers at the time then turned the word into today's "barbecue." For those of us who like all things French, another theory is that the word came from the whole-hog cooking method called "barbe a queue" which means from "head to tail" or, more precisely, "whiskers to tail" in French. For the more fanciful, according to *Bon Appetit* magazine, the word could have come from an extinct tribe in Guyana who "cheerfully spit-roasted captured enemies." *The Oxford English Dictionary* traces the word back to Haiti, while *Tar Heel* magazine suggests that the word "barbecue" came from an advertisement for a whiskey bar, beer- and pool hall that served roasted pig. This establishment was called the BAR-BEER-CUE-PIG. Depending on how much beer you've shared with your marinade, you could probably come up with a few good origin stories yourself. The spelling of barbecue is interchangeable: barbecue, barbecue, BBQ. I've used the latter two versions throughout.

Not Just For Cowboys

According to *Webster's New World Dictionary*, to barbecue is "to roast or broil over an open fire, often with a highly seasoned sauce." To put that definition in practical terms and apply it to real life, I would add "slow-cook at a low temperature" as well.

We have American cowboys to thank for the slow-cook BBQ method. In 1866, a Texas rancher named Charles Goodnight wanted to drive his herd of 2000 cattle from Texas to Denver. Covering that distance in the summer months required that food be prepared along the way, as there was no refrigeration. Out of sheer necessity, Charles Goodnight and his partner invented the first Chuck Wagon. The wagon became a staple on cattle drives and evolved into more elaborate and detailed "kitchens on wheels" as time went on, often featuring closed shelving, hinged pull-down counters for chopping, storage for bedrolls and, of course, the food.

The food consisted mainly of dried black-eyed peas, corn, cabbage and sourdough bread starter. Because the cowboys were most often fed the less desirable cuts of meat – like the brisket – stews seasoned with onions, garlic and chilies became a staple. They would be left to cook for 6-7 hours over an open fire to tenderize the stringy and tough texture of the meat, making it palatable for the hard-working men. Even today that smoky flavor from the grill conjures up visions of the Wild West, a clear, starry sky and an open fire.

CHAPTER SIX

Smoke Signals

From cave man to modern man, humans have a long history with smoking food. There are so many choices now available that you could literally try a different combination of smoking methods every night for a year and not double up.

Low and Slow

The choice between charcoal or gas, tongs or spatulas, misters or beer, is a fairly modern one. There was a time when food needed to be preserved to last for the days when it was scarce, and I have a feeling that folks then probably weren't overly concerned about marinades and rubs. They were, however, concerned about basic survival. Recorded history tells us that humans have been cooking over an open fire long before we could write about it and smoking meat has been a mainstay.

Smoking meat serves three main purposes: To break down fibrous proteins in order to tenderize it, to impart flavor and to cook or preserve it. Here is where the difference between barbecuing in the traditional sense and grilling should be clear.

Barbecuing, smoking or roasting is the practice of cooking meat at a low temperature, slowly, for long periods of time; anywhere from 1 hour to 20 hours or more on indirect heat. Grilling on the other hand, is high and fast; high heat, cooked quickly.

What Do You Smoke?

Well, thank you for asking. I personally prefer a mixture of hardwoods like apple, cherry, oak or hickory, as they allow for longer, more even burning time. These chips can be any variety of the many readily available at your local hardware store or through barbecue specialty stores. I mix 2 part water-soaked woodchips with 1 part dry woodchips. You can also soak them in beer (notice a theme?) or other spirits and herbs. Really, your imagination is the limit.

You can buy metal smoke boxes made for the barbecue, or make one up yourself in a few minutes. Use a large piece of tin foil, place the wet and dry woodchips on it, and fashion it into a packet. Pierce it with a fork making small holes in the top and bottom for the smoke to escape. Put the packet on the grill, under the grilling racks. Bring your barbecue up to a high heat and watch for the smoke. How long you want the smoke to last will determine how much mixture you need. You may need to make up more than one "packet" if the smoke gets low. A steady stream of smoke around your meat will keep the smoke particles moving and avoid creosote from settling on your food making it taste bitter. Creosote is a by-product of burning wood. It forms a tar that is extremely flammable and not too pleasant to consume. Think of the inside of a fireplace, that's creosote. Would you lick that?

As to what food to smoke, you can smoke anything from ham to cheese, however the more traditional choices are meats like brisket, pork ribs and shoulder. Cuts that you wouldn't normally think to cook in an oven, turn into feasts in a slow barbecue.

It's Getting Hot In Here

Now remember, in order to tenderize, flavor and cook your meat, the temperature has to be low. Controlling the heat on a barbecue is not an exact science, however, so your thermometers come in handy about now - *two* to be exact. Use one for the inside of the barbecue and one for the inside of your meat. For the "low" part of this equation, the external heat of the barbecue or smoker should be at around 220F and the internal temperature of the meat should be no lower than 165F. And for the "slow" part you wait and wait . . . and wait. Seriously, patience and a little care needs to be exercised. If your external temperature is too high, your meat will either dry out or become charred – or both. If it's too low, it won't be safe to eat, nor will it be tender, for that matter. However, you won't care about it being tasty or tender if you're visiting the throne room all night because of under-cooked meat.

Eat Your Veggies!

Life expectancy would grow by leaps and bounds if green vegetables smelled as good as bacon. — DOUG LARSON

Buttermilk Potato Salad

BBQ Beets

Celeriac and Apple Salad

Creamy BBQ Scalloped Taters

Crispy Potato Skins with Bacon

Fire-Roasted Tomatoes

Green Salad with Apricots and Blueberries

Green Salad with Red Wine Vinaigrette

Grilled Corn Salad

Grilled Pesto Peppers

Grilled Rosemary Baby Potatoes

Grilled Vegetable Gazpacho in Cucumber Cups

Grilled Vegetable Quesadillas

Marinated Grilled Asparagus

Mushroom Rice

Potato and Watercress Salad

Rainbow Salad

Roasted Plum Tomatoes

Roasted Stuffed Peppers

Rocket Salad with Basil-Oil Mayonnaise Dressing

Smoked Vidalia Onions

Smokey Southwestern Rice

Snow Pea Salad with Lime-Infused Shrimp

Sweet Potatoes with Orange Pecan Butter

Tomatoes Stuffed with Cheese and Vegetables

Tomatoes with Mozzarella Cheese

Watercress Salad with Orange and Tequila Dressing

Yam Potato Tower

They're good for you and over a flame they taste like a treat. Everything from asparagus, to eggplant and zucchini come to life when grilled – honestly!

I've never eaten a vegetable that I didn't like. Well, I guess I should rephrase that. In my adult years, I have never eaten a vegetable that was properly prepared, that I didn't like! Especially when done on the grill. The combination of the smoke, simple seasoning and slight caramelizing really brings the natural flavors up a notch.

How Does Your Garden Grow?

Gardening requires lots of water – most of it in the form of perspiration.
—LOU ERICKSON

While researchers parry back and forth about just how many portions of vegetables one should consume per day, one thing is obvious. Your grandmother was right; vegetables are good for you. Rich in fiber, vitamins and minerals, and beneficial for their high water content, a diet which includes a variety of veggies is simply smart. I would hazard to say that a lot of the fuss with veggies and why people don't like them has to do with the way they are prepared and presented. I wonder if these naysayers have ever had a nice broccoli marinated with a bit of olive oil, balsamic vinegar, salt and pepper lightly grilled on the barbecue? They'd change their mind in a hurry!

There are five elements: earth, air, fire, water and garlic.
—LOUIS DIAT

The word vegetable is actually not a botanical word, but is a culinary term meaning an edible part of a plant that is consumed as sustenance, but which is not a fruit, nut, grain, spice or herb. The practice of growing vegetables for commercial use is a branch of horticulture called "olericulture." (You can thank me for this trivia at your next office party.) Vegetables are usually considered to be savory or non-sweet with the exception of pumpkin and rhubarb. Although I have to say, rhubarb is not something I'd consider sweet on its own! Delicious though it might be with a bit of sugar, in a pie with some strawberries, with a dollop of whipped cream (with a hint of fresh vanilla) on top . . . sorry I digress.

The wonderful thing about vegetables – food from the earth – is the fact that virtually every edible part of a plant is up for consumption and can be divided into five groups:

- *The Flower (Brassicas): cauliflower, broccoli (cruciferous), artichokes*
- *The Seed: corn, peas, beans*
- *Leaf: lettuce, cabbage, spinach*
- *Stalk: celery, asparagus, fennel*
- *Root: carrots, parsnip, turnips*

From there you can sub-categorize and group until you're blue in the face:

- *Shoot Vegetables: asparagus, chicory, bamboo shoot*
- *Onion Family Vegetables: onion, shallot, spring onion*
- *Tubers: potatoes, sweet potatoes, yams*
- *Fruit Vegetables: tomato, cucumber, sweet pepper, avocado*
- *Edible Fungi: mushrooms – all varieties*
- *Seaweeds: Kombu, Wakame, Irish Moss*

Some of the best BBQ veggies

Onions: Spring, Spanish, shallot: you name it, they are all wonderful on the grill. They caramelize beautifully, bringing out their hidden natural sweetness.

Carrots: Cut them to a uniform size, brush with a bit of oil on a medium grill and they'll be sweeter than any carrot you've ever tasted!

Mushrooms: I like all mushrooms, but the Portobello is considered the steak of the mushroom world – sort of like tuna is the steak of the sea! You can eat it straight off the grill on a bun with the same condiments you'd use for your favorite burger.

Corn: Go ahead and leave the husk on! Remove the silk and soak corn in water for about an hour to prevent it from drying out. If you're so inclined you can tie the ends before cooking. Place on a medium grill for 15–20 minutes, turning often to avoid scorching. Delicious!

Yellow squash and zucchini: Those of you who grow zucchini in your garden probably have an overabundance of it! If you can't bribe your neighbors into taking any more and you're looking for a different way to cook it, put it on the grill. Sliced and lightly grilled for 5–10 minutes – it's amazing!

Bell Peppers: The more colors the merrier! Your grill will look like the United Nations. Remove seeds, cut in half lengthwise and grill for about 3–4 minutes. So perfect, so easy!

Potatoes: In jackets, out of jackets, mashed, crushed, whole, sliced, diced – potatoes are wonderful. The carbohydrate-conscious folks have shied away from the lowly tuber, yet sweet potatoes have fewer carbs than the white variety and still offer a great potato "feel." The key to cooking potatoes on the grill is to cook the inside while not burning the outside. Either steamed in foil or sliced on the grill, they are the perfect BBQ food. I love to slice a whole potato in half lengthwise, place the pieces on a large sheet of foil, sprinkle each half with a bit of salt and pepper, add onion slices and a bit of butter. Seal it up in the foil and cook on medium heat, turning regularly for 20–30 minutes. Great with a steak!

I could go on and on and on about veggies, but really give yourself permission to explore. Turnips, radicchio, fennel, parsnips, broccoli, cauliflower – "it's all good!" And best of all, if you have fussy eaters in your midst, grilling disguises some veggies both in taste and appearance. Your resident fusspot might not know that he or she is eating a dreaded broccoli stem! Remember, cook on a medium- to medium-high heat and remove before they turn to mush or ashes.

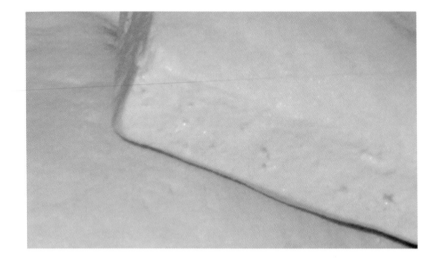

One last thing, for those of us who enjoy a bit of tofu now and again – and for those of us who don't – tofu can also be a great addition to your grilling repertoire. You'll want to look for firm or extra-firm tofu. The silken varieties are great for pureeing, but will not hold up on the grill. Press out excess moisture by weighing tofu down under a plate on paper towels for about 30–60 minutes. Discard remaining liquid. You can then soak the tofu in your favorite marinades, or simply brush with it a bit of oil and seasonings. Soy sauce and sesame oil are wonderful on tofu. Grill on medium heat until browned, about 5 minutes per side. Make sure you oil the grill generously before flipping.

Tip – Freezing tofu will give it a chewier texture and will help it absorb marinades like a sponge. Freeze for at least 36 hours to get the full effect. It's wonderful, I promise!

BUTTERMILK POTATO SALAD

Potato salad: a staple at any family cook-out. But wait until you see how one different ingredient – buttermilk – can improve this tried-and-true.

6 medium baking potatoes, peeled

1/4 red bell pepper, sliced

1/4 yellow bell pepper, sliced

5 hardboiled eggs

1/3 cup chopped sweet pickles (75mL)

2 tbsp sweet pickle juice (30mL)

5 sliced green onions

1 1/2 tsp chives (7.5mL)

1 tsp garlic salt (5mL)

1 tsp freshly ground black pepper (5mL)

Salt to taste

Dressing

1/4 cup sour cream (50mL)

1/2 cup buttermilk (125mL)

2 tbsp chopped fresh chives (30mL)

1 tbsp prepared mustard (15mL)

Directions:

- In a large pot of boiling salted water, cook potatoes for 15–20 minutes or until they are tender. Remove from heat and let stand until cool.

- Combine sliced bell peppers with chopped eggs, pickles, pickle juice and green onions in a bowl.

- Chop cooled potatoes into bite-size pieces. Add potato and chives to bowl, mixing lightly.

Dressing Directions:

- In a separate bowl, combine dressing ingredients and mix well. Add to salad and let stand in the refrigerator for at least 2 hours before serving.

Serves 6

BBQ BEETS

Make sure you wear rubber gloves when you peel the beets! This recipe is so simple and puts a lot of colour and taste on the plate.

4 medium beets, rinsed and trimmed

6 tbsp bottled raspberry vinaigrette (90mL)

1 tsp fresh tarragon, minced (5mL)

1 tbsp olive oil (15mL)

Directions:

* Partially boil the beets in a pot of boiling water (for approximately 15 minutes). They should be a bit firm. Cool, peel and slice the beets into 1-inch thick rounds and set aside.

* Pour the raspberry vinaigrette into a bowl and mix in the fresh tarragon.

* Preheat the barbecue to low heat 250F (125C).

* Using a brush, apply the raspberry dressing to the beets.

* Oil the grill. Place the beets on the grill. Cook for 2 minutes per side, serve and enjoy!

Serves 4

CELERIAC AND APPLE SALAD

Celeriac (also known as celery root) is a special kind of celery grown for its big knobby root. It's mild in taste—think of a cross between celery and parsley—and pairs up nicely with crisp tart Granny Smith apples.

1/3 cup mustard vinaigrette (75mL)

 (see recipe below)

1 celery root, 14–16 ounces (400–500g)

Juice of 1/2 an orange

1/2 cup carrots, sliced into matchsticks (125mL)

1 large Granny Smith apple, cored, quartered and sliced into matchsticks

3 tbsp chopped hazelnuts (45mL)

Mustard Vinaigrette

2 tbsp red wine vinegar (30mL)

2 shallots, finely diced

1 garlic clove, minced

Pinch of salt and pepper

1 tbsp Dijon mustard (15mL)

1/3 cup hazelnut oil (75mL)

2 tbsp chopped chives (30mL)

1 tbsp chopped parsley (15mL)

Directions:

- Peel the celery root as you would an orange, then cut into 1/2-inch (1 cm) thick disks and cut again into matchstick-sized pieces. Place the celery root in a bowl of acidulated water (water with orange juice added) to prevent browning while preparing the remaining ingredients.

- Once dressing has been prepared, strain the celery root matchsticks and toss into large bowl. Add the apple and carrot and mix together.

- Pour dressing on salad just before serving and garnish with chopped hazelnuts.

Mustard Vinaigrette Directions:

- For the vinaigrette, blend the Dijon, red wine vinegar, minced garlic, and diced shallots. Add hazelnut oil until thick. Pour into a bowl and stir in some chopped parsley and chives.

Serves 4

CREAMY BBQ SCALLOPED TATERS

Asiago cheese is the secret to this dish. It's a semi-firm Italian cheese with a sweet nutty flavor and plays nicely off the nip from the cheddar. With two types of cheese, butter AND whipping cream, this is obviously not a diet dish, but worth the splurge.

2 1/2 lbs baking potatoes, sliced (1.2kg)

1 large white onion, sliced

2 tbsp butter (30mL)

1/2 cup asiago cheese, shredded (125mL)

1/2 cup white cheddar, grated (125mL)

1 tablespoon fresh rosemary, chopped (15mL)

1 tablespoon chopped garlic (15mL)

1/2 cup whipping cream (125mL)

Salt to taste

Freshly ground black pepper to taste

Directions:

- Cut the potatoes into 1/4-inch thin slices. Slice onion thinly. Place butter in a saucepan over low to heat to melt.

- Brush some melted butter over a 24-inch square of heavy-duty aluminum foil. Arrange half of the potatoes and half the onion in a single layer (potatoes underneath and onions on top). Brush the layer generously with melted butter and season with salt and pepper.

- Sprinkle the layer with the cheddar and asiago cheeses. Add the remaining onions. Sprinkle freshly chopped rosemary and garlic on top of the onions. Add the last layer of potatoes and brush with more butter.

- Fold the sides of the foil up and carefully pour in the cream. Seal the foil closed with a double fold.

- Preheat the barbecue to medium-high heat 350F (175C). Place the potato package directly over the heat source and cook for 25–30 minutes. Serve as a scrumptious side dish.

Serves 4

CRISPY POTATO SKINS WITH BACON

A spin on a pub favorite. The provolone, along with the bacon, makes it melt in your mouth! By the way, this is a good way to get your kids to eat potato skins, which are loaded with fiber!

6 large russet potatoes (baked for 1 hour
   at 400F (200C) and cooled)

1 cup bacon, cooked and chopped (250mL)

1 tbsp olive oil (15mL)

2 cups provolone cheese, shredded (500mL)

1/4 cup green onions, chopped (60mL)

Salt and pepper to taste

Directions:

- Cut baked potatoes in half, lengthwise

- Scoop flesh from potatoes leaving 1/4 inch in each potato.

- Drizzle potato skins with olive oil. Add salt and pepper to taste

- Sprinkle with green onions, bacon and cheese.

- Preheat barbecue to 220F (104C) or medium-high. Place potatoes over well-oiled grill.

- Cook for 4–5 minutes with lid closed or until cheese has melted and bottoms of potatoes are crispy. Serve with sour cream.

Serves 6

FIRE-ROASTED TOMATOES

Roasting tomatoes brings out their natural sugars and makes them sweet, sweet, sweet. Keep an eye on them though, leave them on the grill too long and you end up with mush!

10 large beefeater tomatoes, halved

4 garlic cloves, finely sliced

2 tsp lavender honey (10mL)

2 tbsp balsamic vinegar (30mL) plus
*   1 tbsp to drizzle (15mL)*

1 tbsp olive oil (15mL) plus 1 tablespoon
*   to drizzle (15mL)*

Salt and black pepper to taste

1 tbsp flat-leaf parsley, chopped (15mL)

Directions:

- Preheat barbecue to 300F (150C) or medium-low heat.

- Place tomato halves cut-side-up on a baking sheet or perforated barbecue tray. Divide garlic slices between the tomatoes and place on top of each tomato half. Drizzle with honey, vinegar and oil. Season the tomatoes with salt and pepper.

- Place the tray of tomatoes on the grill. Roast the tomatoes until very soft and lightly charred (about 30 minutes). Remove tomatoes from the grill and place on a serving platter. Sprinkle with parsley and drizzle with remaining olive oil and balsamic vinegar.

- Serve chilled or at room temperature.

Serves 6

GREEN SALAD WITH APRICOTS AND BLUEBERRIES

I put all kinds of berries in my salads when summer comes around. Arugula is my favourite leaf with a pungent peppery taste and is a classic match for sweet apricots and blueberries.

2 cups white wine vinegar, warmed (500mL)

1 Vidalia onion

1 tbsp coarse salt (15mL)

1/4 cup fresh basil, chopped (60mL)

Juice of 1 lemon

2 tablespoons olive oil (30mL)

1 cup fresh or frozen blueberries (250mL)

1/2 cup sugar (125mL)

4 fresh apricots, sliced 1/4-inch thick

2 bunches arugula, washed

1/3 cup vegetable oil (75mL)

1 lemon

4 wooden skewers soaked in water for 1 hour

Directions:

• Pour the white wine vinegar into a pot over low heat to warm through. Remove from heat.

• Add blueberries, sugar and lemon to warmed vinegar. Let sit for 20 minutes then strain blueberries from flavored vinegar and discard. Whisk in olive oil and season with salt and pepper.

• Cut the onion into paper-thin slices and place them in a shallow baking dish. Sprinkle salt on the onion slices, chop the fresh basil and add it to the dish. Squeeze the lemon juice over the onion and drizzle with 2 tablespoons of olive oil. Cover the dish with plastic wrap and place in the refrigerator for approximately two hours.

• Thread apricot slices onto skewers.

• Preheat the grill to low heat, approximately 300F (150C). Oil the grill and place the apricots skewers on it. Cook for 2 minutes on each side and remove.

• Remove the onions from the refrigerator and pour them into a serving bowl. Add the apricots and arugula and toss.

• Whisk together 1/2 cup of the blueberry dressing with vegetable oil. Pour over salad and toss.

Serves 6

GREEN SALAD WITH RED WINE VINAIGRETTE

Go down to your local farmer's market and bring home a bunch of whatever greens are out there—chickory, romaine, bib, arugula, whatever . . . and don't forget herbs . . . throw in some herbs!

10 cups assorted fresh summer greens (2.5L)

1/3 cup red onion, thinly sliced (75mL)

1/2 cup julienned red pepper (125mL)

1/2 cup julienned yellow pepper (125mL)

8 oz goat cheese (227g)

1/2 cup toasted pine nuts (125mL)

Dressing

1/2 cup red wine (125mL)

3 tbsp grapeseed oil (45mL)

2 tbsp balsamic vinegar (30mL)

1 tbsp Dijon mustard (15mL)

2 tbsp fresh basil, torn or chopped (30mL)

1/2 tsp salt (2.5mL)

1 tsp cracked pepper (5mL)

1 tsp honey (5mL)

Directions:

- In a medium bowl combine Dijon mustard, red wine and vinegars and whisk, then add remaining ingredients and blend. Taste and adjust seasoning if necessary.

- Place the greens, onions and peppers in a large serving bowl and toss gently.

- Drizzle with one third of the dressing. Top the salad with crumbled goat cheese and toasted pine nuts. Add remainder of dressing, toss and serve immediately.

Serves 6

GRILLED CORN SALAD

Served cold or at room temperature, this salad is fantastic! The buttery texture of the avocado combined with the crunchy sweet corn makes your mouth sing.

8 fresh cobs of corn, cleaned, with husks
    pulled back but not removed

5 tbsp fresh lime juice (75mL)

5 tbsp of cooking oil (15mL)

5 tsp garlic salt (25mL)

2 tsp chili powder (10mL)

2 small avocado, peeled, pitted and chopped

1/2 cup chopped red pepper (125mL)

1/2 cup chopped yellow pepper (125mL)

1/3 cup snipped fresh parsley (75mL)

1/2 tsp of salt (2.5mL)

Directions:

- Preheat grill to a medium heat

- In a bowl, combine lime juice, oil and garlic salt. Brush corn lightly with mixture and sprinkle with chili powder. Set remaining mixture aside. Fold the husks back up around the corn.

- Place corn on grill racks and grill for approximately 8–12 minutes (with lid closed) or until corn is tender, turning every few minutes.

- Meanwhile, add avocado, peppers, parsley and salt to remaining lime juice mixture.

- Cut corn kernels from the finished cobs and add to salad and toss to coat evenly. Serve at room temperature or chill and enjoy!

Serves 8

GRILLED PESTO PEPPERS

Store bought pesto is okay, but try making your own this summer when there's lots of inexpensive fresh basil for sale. Nothing in a jar or a bottle tastes as good as what you make at home yourself.

4 red or yellow peppers

2 large garlic cloves, minced

1/4 cup olive oil (60mL)

8 tbsp pesto (45mL)

Salt and freshly ground pepper

Freshly grated buffalo mozzarella

1/2 cup Panko breadcrumbs (Japanese breadcrumbs, which are larger and stay crisp longer than traditional breadcrumbs)

Directions:

- Cut peppers in half lengthways. Scrape out and discard the cores and seeds. Drizzle olive oil, season with salt and pepper and add a few slivers of garlic into the cavity of each pepper.

- Preheat the grill to 375°F/200°C or medium high heat

- Place the peppers on the grill, cavity side up, until charred (approximately 3 minutes)

- Add a spoonful of pesto into each of the peppers and sprinkle with breadcrumbs and cheese.

- Continue to cook peppers until cheese is melted (approximately 3 minutes).

GRILLED ROSEMARY BABY POTATOES

The combination of white and red baby potatoes look great on the plate with those nice grill marks running across the flesh, specked with chopped rosemary. Perfect with steak or chicken.

1 lb baby white potatoes (1kg)

1 lb baby red potatoes (1kg)

1/4 cup olive oil (60mL)

2 tbsp dried rosemary (30mL)

Salt and pepper to taste

Directions:

* Preheat barbecue to 300F.

* Slice potatoes in half. Place in a sealable plastic bag and add remaining ingredients. Place in refrigerator for 1 hour.

* Place on preheated barbecue, either directly on grate or in grill basket and cook for 15–20 minutes or until golden brown and crispy. Serve and enjoy!

Serves 8

GRILLED VEGETABLE GAZPACHO IN CUCUMBER CUPS

Grilling the veggies before making the soup gives this dish a more profound and layered taste (comes from the natural sugars in the veggies caramelizing on the barbecue). Back off on the vodka if you're going to give this one to the kids though . . .

1 Spanish hot banana pepper, diced into
   small pieces

2 cups chopped yellow tomato, peeled
   and seeded (500mL)

1 yellow pepper, small dice

3 green onions, split and diced

3 cucumbers

2 tbsp fresh basil, chopped (30mL)

1 tbsp tarragon (15mL)

1 cup vegetable stock (250mL)
   or chicken stock (250mL)

1/2 tsp salt (2.5mL)

1/2 tsp white pepper (2.5mL)

2 tsp Worcestershire (10mL)

A few splashes hot sauce

1 tbsp sherry vinegar (15mL)

1/4 cup vodka or to taste (60mL) (optional)

Directions:

- Prepare cucumber by cutting into 2-inch rounds. Scoop out the seeds and flesh in the center of the cucumber using a melon baller or spoon. Be careful not to go all the way through the cup. (Place scooped cucumber into a bowl.) Carve out enough of the cucumber to leave a 1/2 inch (8 mm) border, along sides and bottom. You should have 10–12 mini cups.

- Place all of the remaining ingredients in a food processor including the reserved cucumber. Puree until smooth. Adjust seasoning to taste. Add vodka and strain through a colander.

- Chill for 1 hour and up to overnight to develop flavor.

- Pour puree into cucumber cups and serve immediately.

Serves 5-6 appetizer portions

GRILLED VEGETABLE QUESADILLAS

Zucchini and summer squashes can get lost in the grill. One way to prevent that is to cut your zucchinis lengthwise into long, thin slices. These longer slices are not only visually appealing – think grill marks here – but easier to flip and control on the grill.

6 bell peppers, red, green and yellow,
  quartered and seeded

1 Japanese eggplant, sliced into 1-inch
  thick rounds

2 red onions cut into wedges with root intact

2 zucchini, sliced into 1-inch thick rounds

8 tbsp of olive oil (120mL)

14 oz block Monterey Jack cheese (400grams)

2 chipotle peppers, seeded and sliced
  into rounds

1 tbsp of commercial or homemade salsa
  (15mL)

8 soft corn or wheat tortillas

Salt and pepper to taste

Directions:

- Preheat barbecue to a medium heat.

- Toss bell peppers with onions, zucchini and eggplant in a large bowl and drizzle with oil, coating the vegetables well.

- Place peppers, skin side down on preheated grill and cook until seared and browned underneath. Then grill onions, zucchini and eggplants until they have softened slightly and are branded with brown grill marks. Toss all cooked veggies into a bowl.

- Cut cheese into 20 slices and add to roasted vegetables. Add chipotle peppers and mix in salsa, season with salt and pepper to taste.

- Grill tortillas on one side only. Flip, and pile vegetable mixture into the centers of 4 tortillas. When the tortilla browns underneath, put another tortilla on top, cooked side down. Carefully turn the quesadilla over using a wide pizza server with tubular handles and continue to cook until cheese begins to melt.

- Remove from grill with pizza server, serve immediately and enjoy!

Serves 4

MARINATED GRILLED ASPARAGUS

Rosemary and oregano go together like ribs and marinade. They are a perfect combination, and provide a great way to liven up an underappreciated vegetable!

2 lb fresh asparagus with thick stalks (1kg)

1/4 cup of olive oil

2 teaspoons of fresh oregano (10mL)

2 sprigs of fresh rosemary, stems removed

Salt and pepper to taste

Juice of 1 lemon

Directions:

- Preheat the grill for 15 minutes on high

- Wash the asparagus in cold water and pat dry. Snap the tough bottom portion of the fresh asparagus off and discard. Place asparagus stalks into a large, sealable plastic bag. Add the oil and the remaining ingredients to cover asparagus. Let the vegetables marinate for 10-15 minutes.

- Turn one burner off and turn the burners down to medium.

- Drain the marinade and reserve for dipping sauce. Place the asparagus in a foil pouch and seal. Place the pouch on the grill and cook with the lid closed for 10 minutes, turning at least twice.

- Serve the asparagus warm off the grill. Drizzle with fresh lemon juice and season to taste.

Serves 6

MUSHROOM RICE

Think of dried mushrooms as you would tea leaves in that they infuse the vegetable stock with their musty, woodsy flavor. Twenty bucks gets you an amazing rice-cooker that does away with any rice-sticking-to-the-bottom-of-the-pot issues.

3 cups converted rice (750mL)

6 cups vegetable stock (1500mL)

1 tbsp salt (15mL)

1 tsp pepper (5mL)

1/4 cup dried porcini mushrooms (62mL)

1 cup frozen peas (250mL)

Directions:

- Bring all the ingredients except for the peas to a boil and cover. Reduce the temperature and simmer for approximately 15 minutes until light and fluffy.

- Add peas after 10 minutes.

- Keep warm until ready to serve.

Serves 8

POTATO AND WATERCRESS SALAD

Another simple summer salad that emphasizes fresh ingredients and contrasting textures.

1 lb new red and white potatoes (500g)

2 large bunches watercress

Juice of 2 lemons

2 cloves minced garlic

1/2 cup extra virgin olive oil (125mL)

Salt and freshly ground black pepper to taste

Directions:

- Rinse and scrub potatoes and trim stems from watercress.

- Place potatoes in a large saucepan with enough water to cover completely and bring to a boil over high heat. Reduce heat and boil until potatoes are cooked through – about 25 minutes in total. Drain potatoes and set aside to cool.

- Place watercress in a large salad bowl and set aside. In a separate bowl, combine lemon juice, garlic, olive oil and seasonings and whisk together to create vinaigrette.

- Once potatoes are cool enough to handle cut them into quarters and add to watercress. Pour vinaigrette over potatoes and watercress, mix well and serve immediately.

Serves 4

RAINBOW SALAD

All the colours of the rainbow in one salad bowl, plus lots of great flavors and contrasting textures. This is a salad with a big crunch.

1 yellow tomato, cut into 8 wedges

2 red tomatoes cut into 8 wedges

1 cucumber peeled, quartered
lengthwise, seeded and chopped

1 red bell pepper, seeded and julienned

1 yellow bell pepper, julienned

1 small red onion, cut into thin wedges

1 stalk of celery, halved lengthwise
and chopped

6 x radishes, cleaned and cut into disks

1 x jalapeno pepper, seeded and minced

Directions:

- Combine all of the salad ingredients into a large bowl.

- Drizzle with dressing of your choice and serve.

ROASTED PLUM TOMATOES

Plum tomatoes are also known as Italian tomatoes. They have a nice firm flesh which makes them excellent for grilling, then dicing up as a topping on bruschetta.

*8 ripe plum tomatoes stem end removed
   and cut in half lengthwise*
1 tbsp extra virgin olive oil (15mL)
1 tbsp balsamic vinegar (15mL)
Salt and fresh ground pepper to taste

Directions:

- Prepare barbecue for grilling with indirect heat by preheating one side of the grill to 200F (100C) or medium-low heat and leaving the other side of the grill off.

- Drizzle olive oil on tomatoes and season with salt and pepper.

- Place tomatoes on non-heated side of grill and cook for 1 hour.

- Remove tomatoes and drizzle with balsamic vinegar.

- Serve with crusty bread or with a salad.

Serves 8

ROASTED STUFFED PEPPERS

These roasted peppers are a main course in themselves or make for the perfect appetizer at a casual backyard dinner party. Nice thing is you can do all prep work in advance and hang out with your guests.

6 medium red, yellow and green bell peppers

1/4 cup unsalted butter (60mL)

3 tbsp corn oil (45mL)

3 cups corn kernels fresh or frozen (750mL)

1 large white onion chopped fine

1 small jalapeno pepper, chopped fine

1 small eggplant, chopped

1 medium zucchini, chopped

1 tsp white pepper (5mL)

Salt to taste

1 1/2 cups low sodium chicken stock (375mL)

1/2 cup 10% cream (125mL)

1 tsp hot sauce (5mL)

2 cups of dry cornbread crumbs (500mL)

1 egg, lightly beaten

1/4 cup fresh basil, chopped (60mL)

Directions:

- Slice the tops off of the peppers about a 1/2 inch (8 mm) from stems. Remove seeds and cores carefully. Cut a thin slice off of the bottom of each pepper without cutting into the cavity — this will allow them to stand without wobbling.

- Melt butter and oil in a medium size skillet over medium high heat. Add the corn, onion, jalapeno, chopped eggplant and zucchini. Season with salt and pepper. Sauté until fragrant and onions have become slightly translucent; about 5 minutes.

- Add the cream, stock and hot sauce. Cook the vegetable mixture until slightly thickened; about 7 minutes. Remove filling from heat and let cool.

- Stir cornbread crumbs into cooked filling mixture.

- Whisk the egg lightly in a bowl and stir into the filling until well distributed.

- Place peppers on tray and stuff each pepper equally with filling.

- Replace the tops to the peppers and secure with toothpicks.

- Preheat barbecue to 300F (148C) or medium-low.

- Place peppers on the upper bun rack of the grill and allow the peppers to cook for 40–45 minutes. Remove from heat and serve immediately.

Serves 6

ROCKET SALAD WITH BASIL-OIL MAYONNAISE DRESSING

"Rocket" is another word for "arugula." Both are pretty cool names for this peppery tasting lettuce. The leftover basil oil can be used with pizza, pasta, grilled fish or grilled shrimp.

Basil Oil Mayonnaise Dressing

1 1/2 cups basil leaves stripped from their stock (375mL)

3/4 cup of sunflower oil (175mL)

4 tbsp of olive oil (60mL)

1/2 cup mayonnaise (125mL)

1/2 tsp Dijon mustard (2.5mL)

1 tsp lemon juice (5mL)

Salt and white pepper to taste

2 small handfuls of arugula

1/4 cup shallots, thinly sliced (60mL)

1/4 cup dried cranberries (60mL)

Directions:

- For basil oil, place basil leaves in a bowl and pour boiling water over them, leave for approximately 30 seconds until they turn a brighter green. Drain and refresh under cold running water, drain again and squeeze dry with paper towel. Place in a food processor and add both oils and process to a puree.

- Line sieve with cheese cloth and set it over a deep bowl. Pour basil oil puree and leave undisturbed for 1 hour, or until all the oil has filtered through into the bowl. The solids left behind in the sieve can now be discarded.

- Combine mayonnaise with a splash of basil oil. Add Dijon mustard, lemon juice and salt and pepper to taste. Cover well and chill until needed.

- Place cleaned arugula in a salad bowl and add shallots and cranberries. Just before serving toss salad with 1 tablespoon of basil oil mayonnaise dressing. Serve and enjoy!

SMOKED VIDALIA ONIONS

Cola on onions? You bet! It takes caramelizing to another level! Vidalias are one of the sweetest onions around and are worth watching for. Try this recipe with a nice Spanish onion or mini cippollinos when the Vidalia is out of season.

3 large Vidalia onions

Olive oil

1 can of cola

1 cup apple woodchips

Directions:

- Soak apple woodchips in cold water for 30 minutes

- If using a charcoal grill, arrange coals to heat only one side of the grill. If using a gas grill, use only one burner, leaving one side of the barbecue cool. Preheat barbecue to 220F (110C). Drain apple woodchips, place them in a foil pouch, pierce it with holes, and place on the hot side of the grill.

- Slice each onion in half and peel the outer layer. Cut down to, but not through, the base of each onion half in crisscross directions to make an onion "flower."

- Rub a thin coat of oil over the onions and wrap each half in foil. Transfer onions to barbecue, close cover and smoke for 30 minutes.

- Open foil from the top of onions and drizzle with oil and pour cola over top; this will caramelize the onion and give it an amazing taste. Seal foil, close lid and smoke for another 30 minutes or until onion is tender.

Serves 6

SMOKEY SOUTHWESTERN RICE

If you want to add an extra smokey kick to this dish, then get yourself a bottle of liquid hickory smoke and add it to the water you boil the rice in. Excellent!

2 tbsp of cooking oil (30mL)

4 strips bacon, cut into 1/4-inch slivers

1 medium onion, finely chopped

1 medium green bell pepper, stemmed
   seeded and finely chopped

5 cloves garlic, minced

2 tsp dried basil (10mL)

2 tsp fresh thyme (10mL)

Salt to taste

1 tsp freshly ground black pepper (5mL)

3 tbsp tomato paste (45mL)

1/2 tsp sugar (2.5mL)

5 1/2 cups water (or more if needed) (1375mL)

3 cups long grained rice (375mL)

2 tbsp fresh lime juice (30mL)

1 can cooked kidney beans (15oz)

Directions:

- Heat the oil in a large heavy pot over a medium heat. Add bacon and cook until crispy. Add onion, bell pepper, basil, thyme, salt and pepper and cook until onion is golden brown.

- Stir in tomato paste and sugar and cook for approximately 2 minutes.

- Add water and bring to boil.

- Reduce heat to low. Add rice and lime juice and cover and return to a boil. Cook for approximately 15 minutes or until rice is tender. Add a few tablespoons of water if rice needs to continue cooking.

- Stir in kidney beans during the last 3 minutes of cooking. Remove pot from heat and let stand for 5 minutes.

- Just before serving fluff rice and beans with fork and correct seasoning, adding salt and or black pepper as needed.

Serves 8

SNOW PEA SALAD WITH LIME-INFUSED SHRIMP

The biggest mistake most people make in marinating seafood is in the timing. Marinades have an acidic component (in this recipe it's rice vinegar and lime juice) that "cooks" the seafood while it's marinating. Too long and you get rubbery seafood.

18 large tiger prawns (21–25 /lb),

   peeled and deveined

6 bamboo skewers soaked in water for 1 hour

Shrimp Marinade

Juice of 1 lime

1 tbsp rice vinegar (15mL)

2 tbsp honey (30mL)

Pinch cilantro, chopped (60mL)

1 tsp jalapeno pepper, finely chopped (5mL)

1/4 cup peanut oil (60mL)

3 kaffir lime leaves, finely chopped

Directions:

- Combine marinade ingredients for shrimp. Place shrimp in a sealable plastic bag. Pour marinade over shrimp, seal plastic bag and refrigerate for 30 minutes.

- Preheat barbecue to 400F (200C) or high heat, and oil grill.

- Remove shrimp from marinade. Discard the leftover marinade.

- Place 3 shrimp on each skewer.

- Season shrimp with salt and pepper

- Oil grill and place the shrimp on the barbecue for 1–1 1/2 minutes per side or until cooked through.

- Serve with Snow Pea Salad

Snow Pea Salad

4 cups snow peas, cleaned and sliced
    into strips (1L)

1 red pepper, sliced thin

1 yellow pepper, sliced thin

1 red onion, sliced thin

Dressing

1 tbsp peeled and minced ginger (15mL)

2 large garlic cloves, minced

1/4 cup rice vinegar (60mL)

1 tbsp brown sugar (15mL)

1/4 cup vegetable oil (125mL)

Juice of 2 limes

3 tbsp soy sauce (45mL)

4 tbsp dark sesame oil (60mL)

1/4 cup toasted sesame seeds (60mL)

Pepper to taste

Snow Pea Salad Directions:

- Place sliced snow peas in a large bowl. Add peppers and onions.

Dressing Directions:

- Combine the ginger, garlic, vinegar, sugar, oil, lime juice and soy sauce in a small bowl.

- Whisking vigorously, add the sesame oil and pepper to taste.

- Lightly toss the dressing over salad and sprinkle with sesame seeds.

- Serve with Lime-Infused Shrimp

Serves 6

SWEET POTATOES WITH ORANGE PECAN BUTTER

Sweet potatoes have fewer calories than the regular variety of spud. Feel better? Okay, you're going to love this dish, especially the way the honey plays off the orange juice with a kick from the chilis at the end.

6 small sweet potatoes

1/4 cup vegetable oil (60mL)

Orange Pecan Butter

1/2 cup unsalted softened butter (125mL)

2 tsp liquid honey (10mL)

Juice and zest of 2 oranges

1/4 cup chopped roasted pecans (60mL)

1/2 tsp dry mustard (2.5mL)

1/2 tsp dried chili (2.5mL)

Salt and pepper to taste

Directions:

* Preheat barbecue to 220F (104C) or medium heat.

* Scrub sweet potatoes clean and prick all over with a fork. Rub with oil and season with salt and pepper. Wrap with aluminum foil.

* Place the wrapped potatoes on the grill and allow to cook for 2 hours or until potatoes are fork tender.

* Meanwhile, prepare Orange Pecan Butter. Combine ingredients in a small saucepan and cook over low heat for 1 minute.

* Remove potatoes from grill and carefully peel back the foil.

* Slice potatoes lengthways and drizzle with Orange Pecan Butter before serving.

Serves 6

TOMATOES STUFFED WITH CHEESE AND VEGETABLES

Look for big round beefsteak tomatoes that have enough body to act as a bowl for all the other good stuff in this recipe. Slippery, fall-through-the grill onions? Put them on a skewer. Make sure to slice onions about 1/2-inch thick. Push skewer through and thread as many as your skewer will hold. Makes turning them with tongs a snap!

4 large ripe tomatoes

Kosher salt

Stuffing

1 medium red onion, cut crosswise into
    1/3-inch slices

1/2 medium red bell pepper and green
    pepper, stem and seeds removed,
    cut into flat pieces

1 medium zucchini cut lengthways in
    1/3-inch slices.

1 cucumber, cut crosswise 1/3-inch slices

2 tablespoons extra virgin olive oil (30mL)

3/4 cup goat cheese (190mL)

1 tablespoon finely chopped fresh
    basil (15 mL)

1 teaspoon balsamic vinegar (5 mL)

Salt and pepper to taste

Directions:

- Cut a 1/2 inch slice off the top of each tomato. Scoop out the center. Discard.

- Lightly salt the inside of tomatoes and tip upside down over paper towels.

- Preheat grill with one side on medium heat and the other side on medium high.

- Season the onions, peppers and zucchini with salt and pepper and drizzle with oil.

- Place the onions over the medium heat side and grill for 3–4 minute per side, or until nice char marks are achieved.

- Place the zucchini and peppers on the medium high side and grill for 2 minutes per side or until nice char marks are achieved.

- Let cool and cut into 1/2 inch small pieces. Combine the chopped grilled vegetables, cucumber, cheese, basil, and vinegar into a bowl and stir.

- Spoon the vegetable stuffing into the tomatoes.

- Grill the tomatoes on the top warming rack of barbecue until cheese is melted.

Serves 4

TOMATOES WITH MOZZARELLA CHEESE

Garlic and oregano infusing gooey melted mozzarella cheese inside a piping hot sweet fleshy tomato? How do you spell summer eats? To roast garlic, cut the top third off of a whole clove of garlic so that each clove is exposed. Pour a bit of olive oil over it and sprinkle with salt. Loosley wrap it up in tin foil and place on the grill (indirect heat) for about 30 minutes. To remove cloves, squeeze the root.

8 medium tomatoes

4 cloves garlic, thinly sliced

8 tbsp shredded or small chunks of
*   mozzarella cheese (1 tbsp per tomato)*
*   (120 mL)*

8 tsp extra virgin olive oil (40mL)

Salt and fresh-ground black pepper

1-2 tbsp of minced fresh oregano (155mL)

Directions:

- Preheat grill for 10– 15 minutes, with all burners on high.

- Remove and save the top of each tomato (top 1/4 of the tomato). Remove 1/2 of the core from each tomato and discard, leaving a hollowed-out tomato with the base intact.

- Place half of a garlic slice and 1 tbsp of mozzarella cheese into each tomato cavity. Drizzle with olive oil and sprinkle with salt, pepper and oregano.

- Replace tomato tops and grill the tomatoes in a grill plate/basket or on a tray with the cut side of the tomato up. BBQ for 10 minutes or until tomatoes are soft to touch. Serve and enjoy! Great with roasted garlic.

Serves 8

WATERCRESS SALAD WITH ORANGE & TEQUILA DRESSING

Jicama is also known as a "Mexican potato" and can now be found in most major grocery stores. It has a sweet nutty flesh that chops up pretty easily. In this dish it gets matched up with tart tangerine and peppery watercress.

Salad

3 large bunches watercress with
*   tough stems removed*

2 tangerines with membrane removed
*   and sectioned*

3/4 cup diced jicama (175mL)

1/2 cup of mild red radishes thinly
*   sliced (125mL)*

1/4 cup sliced green onions (60mL)

Dressing

1/4 cup fresh orange juice (60mL)

1/4 cup vegetable oil (60mL)

2 tbsp tequila (30mL)

2 tbsp of lime juice (30mL)

2 tsp of honey (10mL)

1 clove of garlic

Directions:

- Combine salad ingredients in a salad bowl, and toss.

- For dressing, combine ingredients in a blender and pulse until mixture is smooth.

- Drizzle the dressing over salad, toss and enjoy!

Serves 4

YAM POTATO TOWER

4 large yams sliced 1/2-inch thick on an angle

Salt and pepper to taste

2 tbsp olive oil (30mL)

Filling

1 cup crumbled goat cheese (250mL)

3 tbsp basil (45mL)

Salt to taste

Pepper to taste

1/2 cup toasted pecans, crumbled (125mL)

Zest of one lemon

Directions:

- Preheat grill to 375F (190C) or medium-high heat.

- Drizzle yams with olive oil, salt and pepper.

- Sear on medium-high heat 1–2 minutes per side or until slightly softened.

- Remove from grill and allow to cool.

- Reduce grill temperature to 325F (162C) or medium-low heat.

- On a tray layer one disk of yam with filling and top with another yam disk. Layer more cheese and top with a third yam disk. Repeat until you have 6 yam towers.

- Place foil on grill and then place yam towers on foil.

- Grill with lid closed for 4–5 minutes or until fully warmed. Serve and enjoy.

Serves 6

What's Your Beef?

The west wasn't won on salad.
–NORTH DAKOTA BEEF COUNCIL ADVERTISEMENT, 1990

Apple-Stuffed Veal with Minty Rub

Beef Brisket

Beef Short Ribs

Cherry wood-Smoked Veal Chops with Apple Brandy Sauce

Mushroom Pecan Veal Chops

Papaya-Glazed Veal Ribs

Seared Beef on Thyme Crostini with Cranberry Chutney

Sirloin Steak with Onion-Garlic Mustard Sauce

Slow-Smoked Beef Ribs

Spicy Beef Skewers with Sour Cream

Veal Chops with a Port and Red Wine Glaze

No, Buffalo wings don't come from buffalos, and "chicken of the sea" isn't chicken at all, for that matter. Confusing? Well, when it comes to beef, there are so many different cuts of meat that are perfect for the grill, that it too can be a bit overwhelming. Learn the basic cuts to diversify your repertoire and beef up your palate.

A Little On The Chewy Side

There is a reason why beef is such a popular choice for the grill, as opposed to say, cottage cheese. First, the animal itself offers an abundance of choices – eight primal cuts (areas of the cow) in all. And of course once you've mastered the art of preparing the many different cuts, the chews you choose will be less chewy to chew (forgive me, I couldn't help myself). Here's a quick – very quick – overview:

Chuck/shoulder: Located right near the neck section of the cow along the side and top running to the fifth rib. Meat from this section tends to be a bit on the fatty side, but flavorful. As it has a lot of connective tissue, it's a popular choice for hamburgers. If not ground, it will need a low-and-slow method for cooking in order to tenderize it.

Rib: The rib cut section sits next to the chuck towards the back of the animal. It starts at the sixth rib and extends to the twelfth. This area produces meat that has a robust beefy flavor with some tenderness to it. Prime rib and rib-eye steaks come from this area.

Short Loin (or loin): The short loin cut comprises of the last rib to the end of the midsection of the animal. Several wonderful choices come from this area. The tenderloin, also known as filet mignon is the most tender cut on the cow and has an extremely mild flavor. Strip steaks, also known as shell steaks, come from here, as do T-bone and porterhouse steaks. The T-Bone and porterhouse both contain a bit of the tenderloin and make for a feast.

Sirloin: Still following along the top sections of the cow, the sirloin contains cuts of meat that are relatively inexpensive. These cuts also tend to be a bit on the tougher side and are suitable for low-and-slow roasting. Top sirloin is usually the suggested choice here.

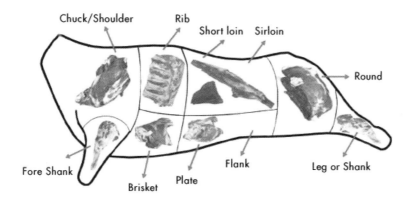

Tip – a little secret is the tri-tip, also called a triangle roast, which comes from the bottom part of the sirloin. It is triangular in shape and usually weighs about 1 1/2 –2 pounds. It can be roasted whole, cut into steaks, or into cubes for kabobs and stir fries. There is only one per cow, so butchers in the past have usually ground it, as there weren't enough for a whole display. Great full taste, but very lean, so it can be dry if not properly marinated or cooked carefully.

Round: Taking up the rear, these cuts are fairly low in fat but can be quite fibrous. Top round is the best of the bunch and with some practice can be seared, then roasted quite nicely.

Flank / Plate / Brisket/Shank: Continuing back to front, these areas make up the smaller underside sections of the animal, where boneless cuts usually on the thicker side are found. The brisket is used a lot in the low-and-slow roasting methods. The plate is usually not sold on a commercial level but rather used in the production of deli meats like pastrami. Flank steak however, is a wonderful choice on the grill – it is meaty flavored and tender.

Whatcha Lookin' At?

You've been standing in the beef section of your grocery store for ten minutes. There's a shopping-cart traffic jam around you and people are giving you dirty looks as they try to squeeze by. What are you looking at? Staring into the display, visions of the perfect barbecue swirl through your head; your family gathered around you gazing up at you adoringly – even your mother-in-law is in awe of your cooking prowess – and then it happens. You break out into a cold sweat as you suddenly realize you don't have a clue which of the dozens of packages to buy.

Choosing fresh, high-quality beef is not as confusing as it would appear. Besides, the government has already very kindly narrowed down most of the choices in quality for us. This is a voluntary program on the part of the meat packers and for our purposes we'll focus on three of the eight grades available.

"Prime" cuts are heavily marbled and therefore very moist, if cooked properly. These cuts are mostly sold to restaurants, butchers and high-end grocers. **"Choice"** cuts are most readily available to the public and have varied levels of marbling. And finally, there are **"Select"** cuts. They have very little marbling and tend to be slightly tougher than the other two grades.

Marbling: Look for meat that is slightly marbled in texture. It helps to impart a rich, robust, distinctly beef flavor. By marbled I mean thin white streaks of fat spread throughout the meat. Avoid big clumps of fat, as it doesn't break down evenly and can be quite tough and unpleasant to eat. Marbling will help the meat stay tender, infusing it with an almost "buttery" feel.

Color: A piece of meat that is a bit older and perhaps tougher in texture tends to be darker in color – a burgundy/brown. Look for brighter reds that are uniform in color throughout.

Purge: The meat should hold water and liquid. If you notice a lot of red juice (blood and water) in the package, it is called purge. This is either the result of freezing that wasn't done properly (perhaps frozen and thawed twice), or meat that is just old. Purged meat will not be as juicy as it should be when cooked.

Smell: If you're buying meat from a butcher, have a quick smell. It should smell mild and non-offensive. If it smells gamey and tweaks your nose even a bit, ask for a different cut.

Firmness: The meat should have a firm feel to it, with a slight spring. If it feels either too hard or too soft, avoid it. It will be either tough and/or flavorless.

I know this seems like a lot to go through for a bit of beef, so if you live in an area with a butcher you trust, either in the grocery store or the shop down the street, I suggest you buy your meat there. You'll be dealing with people who handle the cuts on a regular basis and know what it is you're buying. They'll be able to steer you in the right direction.

The Maillard Reaction (no, not a duck allergy)

Is there anything more appetizing than a steak that is perfectly browned on the outside, especially with those "professional-looking" grill marks that you see in commercials? Still warm, with a shiny buttery look to it – mmm! Well, that browning effect is so desired that it actually has a name. It's called the Maillard Reaction, so named after the French chemist who discovered it a hundred years ago.

The Maillard Reaction occurs when the amino acids, or proteins, mix with the naturally occurring sugars in the meat and together come in contact with high heat. They start a reaction, which turns the meat brown, helping to form a crust on the outside. Almost every self respecting meat eater loves that crust! If your heat is too low, the meat will tend to steam and won't have that brown color to it. Not only is that not as appetizing, but it's also not as flavorful.

Are You Done Yet?

How do you tell if your meat is done? Well, if you're a fourth-generation barbecuer who was born with a silver tong in your hand, you probably go by instinct and experience. But if you're like the rest of us and want a more accurate method, I'd suggest the good old "instant read thermometer." Insert the thermometer into the center of your meat and compare:

Rare 125F (51C)
Medium-Rare 130F (54C)
Medium 140F (60C)

Medium-Well 150F (65.5C)
Well-Done 160F (71C)

Health guidelines suggest that cooking meat to 160F will ensure that all bacteria and pathogens are killed off. Now, although that is very important indeed, the more the meat is cooked, the more the fibers contract and release their juice, which results in a drier piece of meat. Let personal preferences along with the guidelines become your standard.

A Tent In The Kitchen?

A tent in the kitchen? You bet! I know you've been paying attention to everything I've written thus far, so your meat, when it's ready to come off the grill is going to look like sheer perfection. You're going to be hungry and ready to dive in. Hold on a minute, though! Erect a tent I say. That's right, put a piece of foil, or a bowl, or some kind of lid over that piece of art you've just created and wait 5–10 minutes.

As meat is exposed to heat and cooks it coagulates, and the juices from the outside move toward the cooler center of the meat. If you cut your meat right away while it's still piping hot, all the juices from the center will come out onto your plate. Give the meat a rest and let it sit. This will allow some of the fibers to re-absorb the juices and help the meat to be more uniformly juicy. Enjoy!

I am a great eater of beef, and I believe that does harm to my wit.
–WILLIAM SHAKESPEARE

APPLE-STUFFED VEAL WITH MINTY RUB

Apple is a classic combo with veal or pork (you can substitute a nice pork roast for the veal if you'd like). Ask your butcher for the double smoked bacon—it's worth the trip to go and get it.

4 lb boneless veal loin roast (2 kg)

Dry Rub

1/3 cup dried mint (75mL)

1 tbsp fresh rosemary, chopped (15mL)

1/4 teaspoon freshly ground black
   pepper (1mL)

2 tsp garlic powder (10mL)

2 tsp kosher salt (10mL)

Stuffing

1 tbsp olive oil (15mL)

1 large Granny Smith apple, peeled and diced

1/2 lb double smoked bacon, cooked
   and crumbled (250g)

1 tsp lemon juice (5mL)

1 tsp fresh lemon thyme, chopped (5mL)

2 cups sweet apple cider (500mL)

2 rosemary sprigs

Small bunch fresh mint leaves

Directions:

- Combine dry rub ingredients in a small bowl. Toss to mix well.

- Place the veal in a large sealable plastic bag. Add the rub and shake well, coating the veal loin. Remove the veal from the bag and set aside.

- In a non-stick skillet, heat olive oil on medium-high heat. Cook apples for 10 minutes or until softened. Let cool. In a bowl combine the apple, bacon, lemon juice and lemon thyme. Mix well.

- Cut a wide, deep slit into the side of the roast. Stuff the pocket with the apple mixture. Tie the roast at 1-inch (2.5 cm) intervals with heavy string.

- Place a drip pan under the grill of the barbecue, pour in the cider and add the rosemary sprigs and mint leaves. Preheat the barbecue to high heat 325°F/160°C. Leave one burner off. Place roast over grill with no heat. Cook over indirect heat for 2 hours.

- Take veal off the barbecue and let rest for 10 minutes before serving.

Serves 6–8

BEEF BRISKET

Okay, this one takes a bit of effort. But c'mon . . . you get to do your own brisket! As always, experiment with the rub ingredients and come up with your own secret mix.

8 lb beef brisket with 1/2-inch fat cap (4kg)

12 cups apple woodchips

Meat injector needle

Dry Rub

1/2 cup brown sugar (125mL)

2 tbsp chili flakes (30mL)

1 tsp nutmeg (5mL)

1 tsp dried thyme (5mL)

1 tsp oregano (5mL)

2 tsp ground cinnamon (10mL)

1 tsp ground ginger (5mL)

1 tsp coriander (5mL)

2 tsp dry mustard (10mL)

1 tbsp ground black pepper (30mL)

Marinade

1/4 cup apple cider (60mL)

1 tbsp cider vinegar (15mL)

1/4 cup beef broth (60mL)

1 tsp hot sauce (5mL)

1 tsp dried mustard (5mL)

2 tsp pepper (10mL)

1 tsp onion powder (5mL)

1/4 cup melted butter (60mL)

Directions:

- Combine dry rub ingredients and rub into brisket.

- Combine marinade ingredients in a large measuring cup.

- Fill meat injector needle with marinade and inject the rub-covered beef brisket throughout (follow manufacturer's instructions).

- Cover with plastic wrap and refrigerate overnight or up to 24 hours

- Soak 8 cups of apple woodchips in water.

- Build a smoke pouch by squeezing the excess water from 2 cups (500mL) of wet woodchips and place on a large piece of aluminum foil. Place 1 cup (250mL) of dry woodchips on top and mix them together. Close foil around chips to make a sealed package. Using a fork, puncture holes in both sides of the pack to allow smoke to flow through and infuse the meat. Make a total of 4 foil pouches.

- Place drip pan underneath one side of grill. Place smoke pouch on the opposite side. Turn heat on under the smoke pouch to 350F (175C). Close lid and wait for smoke.

- Place brisket on cool side of grill over the drip pan. Close lid. Allow brisket to slowly smoke for 8 hours, change smoke pouches when smoke dissipates (approximately every 2 hours).

- Remove beef brisket from heat, cover with aluminum foil and allow to rest for 15 minutes. Carve against the grain and serve on crusty buns with mustard & pickles.

Serves 8

BEEF SHORT RIBS

Once upon a time, beef short ribs were cheap, cheap, cheap. Not so much any more because everyone wants to do them now. But they are SO worth the effort.

4 beef short ribs, bone in

Dry Rub

1 tbsp Five Spice Powder

1/3 cup of brown sugar (83mL)

3 tbsp of garlic salt (45mL)

3 tbsp celery salt (45mL)

Five Spice Powder

1 tbsp cinnamon

1 tsp ground cloves

1 tbsp ground star anise

1 tbsp freshly ground pepper

2 tsp onion powder

3 cups of woodchips (cherry or apple)
  (750mL)

Directions:

- Combine all of the rub ingredients in a large bowl. Rub half of the rub mixture into the ribs and reserve the other half of the rub for use the next day. Place the ribs in a large plastic bag and refrigerate overnight.

- A half hour before you plan to put the ribs on the grill, remove them from the plastic bag and apply the remaining rub from the night before, leaving approximately 2 tablespoons to sprinkle on the ribs while they smoke.

- Let the ribs stand for half an hour to come to room temperature. This will ensure that they cook evenly on the grill.

- Place 1 cup of the woodchips in cold water to soak for half an hour.

- If your grill has several grates, remove one on the far side and set it aside. Preheat the grill to high heat – approximately 400–450 F (200–225C).

- Squeeze the excess water from the soaking woodchips and place in the center of a large piece of tin foil. Add the remaining 2 cups of dry woodchips. Fold the aluminum foil around the chips to create a sealed pouch. Using a fork, poke holes in the package on both sides to allow the smoke to filter through.

- Place the smoke package directly over the flame on the far side where the grate has been removed. Close the lid and wait for smoke to start building in the barbecue.

- Once smoking has begun, lower the heat under the woodchip pouch and turn the heat off on the other portions of the grill. Wait for the temperature to reach approximately 200F (100C).

- Place the ribs on the grates where the heat is off. Close the lid and leave to smoke with indirect heat for approximately 4 hours. After 11/2– 2 hours flip the ribs and sprinkle with remaining rub mixture.

- After 4 hours, the ribs should have a crispy, delicious exterior and the meat should be almost falling off the bone.

Serves 4

CHERRY WOOD-SMOKED VEAL CHOPS WITH APPLE BRANDY SAUCE

Make sure you get a nice smoke going and have extra packs of woodchips ready to go. Low and slow is the order of this day!

10 veal loin chops, 1-inch thick (16mm)

Marinade

1/2 cup Calvados (125mL)

5 cloves garlic, crushed

4 tbsp olive oil (45mL)

1 tbsp fresh oregano (15mL)

1 tsp fresh thyme, chopped (2.5mL)

1/4 tsp freshly ground pepper (1.25mL)

1/2 fennel bulb, sliced thinly, divided in two

6 cups (1L) cherry woodchips

Directions:

- Combine all the marinade ingredients into a bowl and mix to combine. Slice the fennel and add half to the marinade. Reserve the other half for the smoking pouch. Place the veal in a sealable plastic bag and pour marinade over top. Seal the bag and toss to ensure the veal is well coated with marinade. Refrigerate for 6 hours or overnight.

- Remove the veal from the marinade and allow the meat to come to room temperature.

- Place 4 cups (750 mL) of cherry woodchips (for a gas grill or all the woodchips if using a charcoal grill) into water to soak for 1 hour.

- Prepare the barbecue for smoking. Preheat the barbecue to 400F (200C) or high heat on one side, leaving the other side off. Remove barbecue grate on heat side.

- To make a smoke pouch, squeeze the excess water from the woodchips and place 2 cups in the center of a large piece of foil. Add 1 cup dry chips, the remainder of the sliced fennel and mix (makes 2 pouches). Close the foil around the chips sealing the package. Using a fork, poke holes in both sides of the package. Place 1 smoke pouch directly over high heat source of the grill, close the lid and wait for smoke. If using charcoal, squeeze the excess water from the chips and sprinkle the chips directly into the fire bed.

- When the smoke has filled the cavity of the barbecue, open the lid and place the veal over the "off" side of the grill. Close the lid.

- Smoke the veal for 1 hour and 15 minutes, changing the smoke pouch half way through cooking or when necessary. Remove veal and loosely cover with foil. Let meat rest 5 minutes before serving.

Serves 6

MUSHROOM PECAN VEAL CHOPS

These chops are even better if you let them marinate overnight. Ask your butcher to cut the chops for you "bone on". It looks better when they hit the plate.

4 veal chops, 1-inch-thick each, about
*   12 ounces (350g)*

Marinade

1/2 cup white wine (125mL)

Juice of 1 lemon

3 sprigs sage, chopped

Splash of walnut oil

Pepper to taste

Pecan and Mushroom Dry Rub

1/2 cup dried wild mushrooms (125mL)

1/2 cup pecans (125mL)

2 tbsp dried oregano (30mL)

Salt and pepper to taste

Directions:

* Combine marinade ingredients in a small bowl. Place the veal into a sealable plastic bag, pour the marinade over top, make sure the meat is covered entirely and refrigerate for at least 1 1/2 hours.

* To prepare the rub, in a blender or a coffee grinder, grind the mushrooms to fine dust. Let the dust settle a bit and add the remaining ingredients to the blender or grinder. Combine long enough to make a coarse meal out of the pecans. Pour into a small bowl and rub onto the veal.

* Grill at 350F (175C) for 8 minutes on each side. Serve and enjoy!

Serves 4

PAPAYA-GLAZED VEAL RIBS

Yes, veal ribs. You don't see them very often but they are amazing. Watch your butcher's face light up when you ask for them. He'll know you're a real BBQ god. If you can't find papaya purée, then papaya juice will do just as well.

2 x 5 lb racks of veal ribs (2 x 2.5 kg)

9 cups apple woodchips (2 litres)

Marinade

6 whole green onions

3 tbsp fresh thyme leaves (45mL)

1/2 tsp ground allspice (2.5mL)

1 tsp salt (5mL)

1 1/2 tsp ground black pepper (7.5mL)

1 tsp nutmeg (5mL)

1 tsp cinnamon (5mL)

4 cloves garlic, finely minced

2 tbsp finely minced ginger (30mL)

*1 scotch bonnet pepper, finely minced,
    seeds removed*

1 cup papaya purée (250mL)

4 tbsp light soy sauce (60mL)

2 tbsp cider vinegar (30mL)

1/2 cup vegetable oil (125mL)

1/2 cup dark rum (125mL)

Juice of 1 lime

Directions:

- In a food processor combine all marinade ingredients and process until a smooth paste is achieved. Set aside 1/2 cup (125mL) of the marinade for basting.

- Place veal ribs on a large, non-reactive tray and pour marinade over top. Turn veal to ensure all meat is covered.

- Cover with plastic wrap and place veal in the refrigerator to marinate overnight.

- Place 6 cups (1.5L) of the woodchips to soak for 1 hour.

- Build three smoke pouches: lay out 3 sheets of aluminum foil. Build a smoke pouch by squeezing the excess water from 2 cups (500mL) of wet woodchips and place on a large piece of aluminum foil. Sprinkle some rum over wet chips. Place 1 cup (250mL) of dry woodchips on top and mix them together. Wrap the foil up loosely to create a square pouch. Using a fork, poke holes in the foil to allow the smoke to escape.

- Remove barbecue grill rack from one side of the barbecue. Insert the smoke pouch and turn the heat under the smoke pouch to 400F (200C) or high heat and close lid. Leave the other side of the barbecue off. Wait for smoke.

- Once the cavity of the barbecue is filled with smoke, reduce heat to 220F (104C) or low heat.

- Remove the ribs from the marinade and pat dry.

- Place ribs on cool side of barbecue, opposite the smoke pouch. Close lid on barbecue and check temperature; it should read 220F (104C). Allow the ribs to smoke for 3 hours. You will have to change the smoke pouch every hour.

- Baste with reserved marinade every 30 minutes.

- Once ribs are fork-tender, baste again with remaining marinade. Place ribs on a tray and tent loosely with foil and allow the ribs to rest for 15 minutes before slicing.

Serves 6–8

SEARED BEEF ON THYME CROSTINI WITH CRANBERRY CHUTNEY

This is an elegant combination of flavors – cranberries and fresh thyme!
Great for any dinner party. Pass this around with drinks before everyone sits down
for the main event.

1 center-cut beef tenderloin, sliced into

    1/2-inch portions (8mm)

Salt and pepper

1 tsp dried basil (5mL)

2 tbsp olive oil (30mL)

Cranberry Chutney (recipe follows)

Crostini

1 French stick sliced into 1/2-inch slices (8mm)

1/4 cup of softened butter (60mL)

2 tbsp fresh thyme, chopped (30mL)

Salt and pepper to taste

Cranberry Chutney

3/4 cup sundried cranberries, chopped

    (175mL)

2 tbsp chopped shallot (30mL)

1 tsp crushed tomato (5mL)

4 cloves roasted garlic

1/4 cup honey (60mL)

1 tbsp balsamic vinegar (15mL)

Directions:

- To make crostini, mix butter, thyme, salt and pepper together in a small bowl

- Slice bread into 1/2-inch (8mm) slices and spread evenly with butter mixture. Place on tray.

- To prepare beef, sprinkle slices with salt, pepper and dried basil. Drizzle with olive oil to coat.

- Preheat barbecue to medium-high heat 375F (190C). Oil grill.

- Place the tenderloin slices on grill and cook for 1 minute. Flip and continue to cook for 1 minute or until desired doneness. Remove from grill, loosely cover with foil and let rest 4 minutes.

- Place bread slices on bun rack and cook for 2 minutes until warm and slightly crisp.

- Place beef on bread slices and top with cherry chutney.

Cranberry Chutney Directions:

- In a small bowl mix together all ingredients until well combined.

- Refrigerate for 1–2 hours.

Serves 16 appetizer portions

SIRLOIN STEAK WITH ONION-GARLIC MUSTARD SAUCE

BIG TIP: Always cook your meats with the bone in whenever you can. There's tons of flavor in that bone that insinuates itself into meat as it cooks. And remember, your marinade is only as good as the ingredients you use, so don't cheap out on the wine.

Remember to sear your meat quickly on either side, then turn down the heat and let it cook through to your predetermined temperature. If you're using your instant-read thermometer and it's telling you that your steaks are good only for the garbage pail, I can help:

- Insert the tip of the sensor of your thermometer through the SIDE of the meat NOT from the top. The sensor might not be located directly at the tip of the thermometer; therefore the sensor won't be in the center of your meat.

- Ensure your sensor isn't resting against the bone. You won't get an accurate reading.

- Be sure to check each steak – not all are created equal!

1 x 3 lb sirloin steak, bone-in

2 tbsp olive oil (30mL)

Salt and pepper to taste

Marinade

1 cup red wine (250mL)

1 tbsp cracked black pepper (15mL)

2 rosemary sprigs, coarsely chopped

3 cloves garlic, coarsely chopped

1/4 cup olive oil (60mL)

Directions:

- Place marinade ingredients into bowl and mix well. Place the steak in a sealable plastic bag and pour the marinade over steaks to coat. Seal the bag and refrigerate for 3 hours.

- Pre-heat barbecue to 375F (190C) or medium-high.

- Remove steak from marinade and pat dry. Allow steak to come to room temperature. Drizzle with olive oil and sprinkle with salt and pepper.

- Oil the barbecue grill. Cook steak for 6 minutes, turn 45 degrees and cook for another 6 minutes.

Onion-Garlic Mustard Sauce

2 medium onions, chopped

4 cloves garlic, minced

1/2 lb double-smoked bacon (250mL)

2 tbsp cider vinegar (30mL)

2 tbsp grainy mustard (30mL)

1 tbsp pure maple syrup (15mL)

*1/2 tsp jalapeno, chopped, seeds
    removed (5mL)*

Salt and pepper to taste

1 tsp Tabasco sauce (5mL)

- Flip steak and cook for an additional 6 minutes, turn steak 45 degrees and finish cooking for 6 more minutes (for medium-rare).

- Remove steak and cover with aluminum foil. Let rest for 5 minutes.

- Slice steak into desired portion-sizes and serve with Onion-Garlic Mustard Sauce.

Onion-Garlic Mustard Sauce:

- In a medium skillet, sauté double-smoked bacon, garlic and onions over medium-high heat. Sauté until bacon is crisp and onions are dark brown.

- Add cider vinegar and cook for 40 seconds, reduce heat to low, add the remaining ingredients, and allow sauce to simmer for 15 minutes.

Serves 4

SLOW SMOKED BEEF RIBS

More juicy, tender beef ribs. Have your butcher separate the ribs for you (as opposed to a whole rack) and go to town. The sauce recipe below is really basic, so go through the fridge, pantry, and liquor cabinet and throw in anything else you think will taste great.

2 racks of beef ribs

9 cups hickory woodchips (2L)

Dry Rub

1 tbsp Cajun spice (30mL)

1 tsp thyme (5mL)

3 tbsp brown sugar (45mL)

1 tbsp dry mustard (15mL)

1 tbsp ground ginger (15mL)

2 tbsp onion powder (10mL)

2 tsp garlic powder (10mL)

1 tbsp kosher salt (15mL)

2 tbsp cracked black pepper (10mL)

Beef Rib Sauce

1 bottle commercial BBQ sauce

1 tbsp Worcestershire sauce (15mL)

1 tbsp Dijon mustard (15mL)

1 tsp chili powder (5mL)

1 tbsp lemon juice (15mL)

Splash of hot sauce

Directions:

- Combine rub ingredients in a small bowl. Rub the mixture vigorously and evenly over beef ribs. Place beef ribs in a large, sealable plastic bag and place in fridge for 5 hours or overnight.

- Prepare rib sauce by mixing ingredients in a bowl. Cover and refrigerate until needed.

- Place 6 cups of the woodchips in water and soak for 1 hour.

- Build a smoke pouch by squeezing the excess water from 2 cups (500mL) of wet woodchips and place on a large piece of aluminum foil. Place 1 cup (250mL) of dry woodchips on top and mix them together. Close the foil around the chips to make a sealed foil package. Using a fork, puncture holes in both sides of the foil pack to allow the smoke to flow through and infuse the meat. Repeat twice more to make a total of three pouches.

- Remove one side of the grill grate and insert one smoke pouch.

- Prepare barbecue for grilling with indirect heat by preheating one side of the grill to 400F (200C) or high heat and leaving the other side of the grill off.

- Close lid and wait for smoke. Once you have smoke, lower heat under smoke pouch to 250F (120C) or medium-low heat.

- Place beef ribs on cool side of grill, opposite from the smoke pouch. Close lid and leave to smoke for 2 1/2 hours or until meat is tender enough to fall off the bone. Change smoke pouch every 45 minutes.

- During the last 20 minutes of cooking, baste with rib sauce. Serve with any remaining sauce.

Serves 8

SPICY BEEF SKEWERS WITH SOUR CREAM

This is a fun recipe because you form the ground hamburger into sausage-like torpedoes around the skewer. Remember to soak the skewers for a while so they don't burn on the grill.

2 lbs ground beef (1kg)

1 medium onion, grated with box grater

5 garlic cloves, chopped extra fine

2 tsp paprika (10mL)

1 tsp dried oregano (5mL)

1/2 tsp ground cumin (2.5mL)

1 tsp cracked black pepper (5mL)

2 tsp salt (10mL)

2 tbsp vegetable oil (30mL)

Additional salt and pepper to taste
    if necessary

2/3 cup sour cream (165mL)

8 bamboo skewers at least 10-inches long

Directions:

- Soak bamboo skewers for 1 hour in cool water.

- Place the ground beef, grated onion, chopped garlic and spices into a large bowl. Add salt and pepper and mix well.

- Divide mixture into 8 equal-sized portions. Using your hands, mold each portion around a skewer, shaping it into a sausage, about 8 inches (20cm) long (oil hands to stop the meat from sticking).

- Preheat the grill to 375F (190C) or medium-high.

- Season the skewers with salt and pepper and drizzle with oil.

- Oil the barbecue grill.

- Place the skewers directly on the oiled grill. To prevent the skewer ends from burning, place a sheet of aluminum foil beneath the uncovered part of the wooden skewers.

- Grill the skewers for 8–10 minutes, turning every 2 minutes. The meat will be golden brown with a slightly crispy exterior. Remove from grill and loosely tent with foil to keep warm before serving.

- Serve with sour cream.

Serves 8

VEAL CHOPS WITH A PORT AND RED WINE GLAZE

This glaze has got the grape going on in four ways: in the port, the wine, the jelly and the vinegar. It has an amazing depth of flavour that will leave your guests swooning.

6 veal chops, 3/4 pound each

1/4 cup of olive oil

2 tbsp of chopped fresh sage (30mL)

Port and Red Wine Glaze

1/2 bottle (375mL) dry red wine

1/2 cup port (125mL)

1/4 cup red wine vinegar (125mL)

1/2 cup of grape jelly (125mL)

1 tsp of salt (5mL)

1 tbsp minced garlic

Directions:

- Place the veal on a tray. Drizzle with the oil and sprinkle fresh sage. Refrigerate for 3 hours.

- Combine the ingredients for the glaze in a saucepan. Bring to a vigorous boil and simmer until it reduces to 1 1/4 cups. This may be done in advance and refrigerated until ready to use.

- Bring the veal chops to room temperature.

- Brush the grill with vegetable oil to help avoid sticking. Lay the chops over high heat to char. Once you have char marks on either side of the chops, lower the heat to 350F and continue to cook. Brush with the glaze every 5 minutes for approximately 12–15 minutes. Grill the veal until it reaches an internal temperature of 150F (66C). It should still be pink inside.

- Place any remaining glaze back over heat, simmer and stir in the butter. Season with salt and pepper and drizzle the sauce over the veal chops. Serve and enjoy!

Serves 6

This Little Piggy

A cat will look down to a man. A dog will look up to a man.
But a pig will look you straight in the eye and see his equal.
–WINSTON CHURCHILL

Apple-Smoked Pulled Pork

Baby Pork Back Ribs

Bourbon-Glazed Smoked Spareribs

Country Style Ribs

Dark-Beer-Marinated Pork Tenderloin

Dry Caribbean Baby Back Ribs

Grilled Fresh-Herb-Brined Pork Chops

Prosciutto-Wrapped Figs Stuffed with Blue Cheese

Pulled Pork Picnic Roast

Root Beer Ribs

Rubbed Smoke Pork Tenderloin Cajun-Style

Slow-Smoked Thai Ribs

Smokey Canadian Bacon

Stuffed Pork Tenderloin with Golden Raisin Glaze

"To Live For" Pancetta and Potato Package

Get yourself to the market – pork is lean meat after all. Easy to prepare, pork is a natural for the flame, from the chops to the ribs. And with so many choices, it will blow your house down.

Most Popular Pig

This may be a bit surprising to North Americans: pork is the most consumed meat product in the world. That's right, *the world*. It's economical to produce and purchase and much of the animal can be used in one way or another, making it extremely versatile for all budgets. Pork has suffered a bit of a bad rap, and yes, at one time perhaps there was reason for it. It was high in fat relative to other muscle meats and contained its share of bacteria. However, this little piggy has gone on a diet and cleaned up its pen!

The pork industry went through a dramatic makeover at the end of the 1970s, when North Americans became more health conscious. Responding to public demands for leaner, cleaner cuts of meat and the creation of regulatory Pork Boards, pork producers systematically started to breed and raise pigs to be leaner and healthier – 31% to 50% leaner for most cuts (other than bacon), depending on which source you read. While that is certainly beneficial to our overall health, it unfortunately comes with a price – taste.

The less marbling there is throughout the meat, the less natural flavor and tender, buttery texture. A pork chop, for example, in the 1960s would fry up in a pan to create a veritable feast. Nowadays that pork chop can get really dry really quickly thanks in part to its leanness and also to our fear of undercooking (which I'll get into later).

Chop, Chop

Just like cows, pigs are divided into primal cuts; however, unlike the larger bovines, which are divided into eight cuts, there are only four on the swine:

Shoulder: This area gets a lot of exercise, so it tends to be tough. The low-and-slow method applies to all cuts here. Popular choices from the shoulder: Boston butt, roast or steak; ground pork for sausage; blade steak; and ham hocks. Ham hocks are used mainly for flavoring.

Loin: Located in the middle of the animal, along the top of the spine, this area is extremely lean and can therefore be dry. However, a lot of popular cuts come from here including ribs, tenderloin, pork chops, sirloin and whole loin (butterfly chops).

Leg: The leg is also referred to as ham. We're all familiar with a beautifully prepared ham during the holidays – cooked to perfection with that low-and-slow method.

Belly: Along the underside; this area is the fattiest section of the pig. This is where your succulent bacon comes from along with those cherished spareribs and back ribs.

Stick Out Your Tongue And Say AHH!

All meat products contain bacteria; it's just a fact of life. Pork, however, contains one specific bug (worm, actually) that makes pork-lovers leery. The parasite is called *Trichinella spiralis* and the condition it causes is called trichinosis. Once this worm larva is consumed, the first symptoms are nausea, diarrhea, vomiting, fatigue, fever, and abdominal discomfort. If you're particularly unlucky, headaches, fevers, chills, a cough, eye swelling, aching joints, muscle pains and itchy skin can follow. Thankfully these symptoms are rare. In fact, since 1997, only twelve cases of trichinosis per year on average have been reported in North America. Both breeders and inspectors have made pork a healthier alternative, and although eating pork no longer has any stigma attached to it, it is important to make sure your pork is cooked to at least 160F.

The Good Student

Like beef, pork inspection is quite comprehensive. Every animal for human consumption is inspected for contamination of the intestine, and if passed, given a seal of approval.

The grading system – also much like beef – is voluntary; however, it only has two grades. The first is Acceptable. Acceptable grades are sold to grocery stores and restaurants. Next is Utility. Meats deemed Utility are used in processed foods and are not sold for public consumption.

Will That Be Red or White?

Is it fact or fiction that pork is white meat? Drum roll please . . . the answer is fiction. Pork is red meat. As a matter of fact, all livestock are considered red meat. So why do we think of pork as "the other white meat"? Because of an excellent marketing campaign driven by the U.S. National Pork Board, which goes all the way back to 1987. That slogan capitalized on the fact that pork does indeed turn a whitish color when cooked, comparing it to the perceived "healthier" choices of chicken and turkey.

What makes red meat red? One of the proteins in meat is called myoglobin, which receives oxygen from red blood cells. The amount of myoglobin in an animal's muscles makes up the color of the meat. Beef and pork have more myoglobin then say, chicken and are therefore considered red meat.

To The Market

Okay you're back in the meat section; this time looking for that perfect serving of pork for your meal. It's not complicated at all:

Marbling: Just like with beef, a little bit of even marbling (white fat) throughout is imperative for both taste and texture. Stay away from cuts with more than 1/4 inch of fat on the outside. Ask your butcher to trim it for you, or do it yourself, for that matter.

Firmness: The meat should be firm to the touch, never hard or grisly feeling.

Color: Look for cuts that are a grayish pink color.

Smell: Avoid anything that smells rancid or "off." Fresh pork should have a mild smell.

Fresh not Frozen: Stay away from pork that has been frozen, as it will tend to be dry and stringy. Juices in the bottom of the package will be your warning sign.

Too Hot To Handle

A good rule for cooking pork and all meat products is to bring the internal temperature up to 160F for medium and 170F for well done. This will insure that all parasites and other bacteria are gone.

Now, with all the things to watch out for, I'm not surprised if you're feeling a little sheepish about cooking pork. But really, common sense applies here. Just like all meats, you want to avoid cross-contamination. In other words, never use utensils and vessels on your cooked meat that have touched your raw meat. Disinfect cutting boards, counter and sink surfaces when done. Never partially cook meat to cook at a later date and always store meat, whether cooked or raw, in the fridge. See, that's pretty simple!

If you're brushing a marinade on your pork, which is an excellent choice for ribs, and you want to use the extra marinade for dipping sauce, you must boil it for 5 minutes first. Better yet, set aside some of the marinade when you make it and you'll have no worries.

The Pink Debate

Sometimes freshly cooked pork will have a pink tint in the center. Because of the worry of *trichinosis* we have become guarded about that pink. "Have no fear," I say. As long as the internal temperature has reached 160F it should be safe. The pink could also be the result of using a marinade.

'Twas an evening in November,
As I very well remember,
I was strolling down the street in drunken pride,
But my knees were all a'flutter
So I landed in the gutter,
And a pig came up and lay down by my side.
Yes I lay there in the gutter
Thinking thoughts I could not utter,
When a colleen passing by did softly say,
"Ye can tell a man that boozes
By the company he chooses"
At that, the pig got up and walked away.
  –ANONYMOUS

APPLE-SMOKED PULLED PORK

The "Boston Butt" is a big fatty cut that begs for long, slow cooking. The fat fairly melts away, dripping through the meat and infusing it with lots of taste and tenderness. Remember, fat is taste, fat is your friend. Everything in moderation (sort of) of course. Get yourself some nice sourdough buns and a bunch of condiments and load up the sandwiches with lots of pulled pork.

1 Boston Butt (bone-in pork shoulder roast),
    5–6 lb (2.5–3 kg), covered with a layer
    of fat 1/2–1-inch thick
6 cups apple woodchips

Dry Rub

1/2 cup of brown sugar (125mL)

1/2 cup of kosher salt (125mL)

1/3 cup of paprika (84mL)

3 tbsp of black pepper (45mL)

4 tsp of garlic powder (20mL)

2 tsp of thyme (10mL)

2 tsp of coriander (10mL)

2 tsp of cayenne (10mL)

2 tsp of dry mustard (10mL)

Basting Liquid

Spicy Vinegar-Based BBQ Sauce (page 226)

Directions:

- Combine dry rub ingredients in a bowl.

- Put on a pair of rubber or plastic gloves to protect your hands from discoloring. Apply the rub to the pork with medium to light pressure. Rub the mixture into the pork and ensure that the entire surface is well spiced.

- Place the pork butt into a large plastic bag to rest for 5–8 hours.

- Place 2 cups of the apple woodchips in water and soak for 1 hour.

- Drain half (1 cup) of the wet woodchips and squeeze the excess water out. Spread them evenly on a large piece of tin foil. Place 2 cups of the dry woodchips on top and mix them together. Close the foil around the chips to make a sealed foil package. Use a fork and puncture holes in the top and bottom of the foil package to allow the smoke to flow through and infuse the meat.

- When the pork has finished marinating, let it rest for approximately 30 minutes to bring it to room temperature. This will ensure that it cooks evenly.

- Remove the grill top and place the woodchip package directly over high heat to the far side of the barbecue. Once smoke is visible, turn the heat down to a medium-low heat (220°C).

- Place the pork on the opposite side of the grill from the smoke package. Use indirect heat to smoke the pork by ensuring that there is no direct heat under the meat. The only heat on should be the burner underneath the smoke package.

- Close the lid and allow the pork to cook for 1 hour before opening the lid. After 1 hour, lift the lid and baste the meat quickly. Baste every 20-30 minutes.

- If you would like a more intense smokey flavor on the pork, after 2 hours, build another smoke package using the remaining wet and dry woodchips and swap it for the now finished first package. If not, continue to cook over indirect heat for another 2 hours.

- Continue to cook for the remaining 2 hours, basting every 20–30 minutes. The meat is done when the pork pulls away easily from the skin.

- Perfect in buns and served as sandwiches.

Serves 4

BABY PORK BACK RIBS

The orange zest, mixed with the sesame oil and soy sauce is such a wonderful, silky combination—multilayered yet still uncomplicated.

3 full racks of baby pork back ribs,
8 ribs each
Mildly flavored vegetable oil to brush
on the cooking rack

Barbecue Sauce

1/2 cup Hoisin sauce (125mL)
1/4 cup plum sauce (60mL)
1/2 cup oyster sauce (125mL)
1/4 cup red wine vinegar (60mL)
1/3 cup honey (75mL)
2 tbsp dark soy sauce (30mL)
2 tbsp dry sherry (30mL)
2 tbsp sesame oil (30mL)
1 tbsp Sambel Olek (15mL)
1 tsp of Five Spice Powder (5mL) (Page 74)
1 tbsp of pepper (15mL)
1 tbsp of finely grated orange zest (15mL)
8 cloves of finely minced garlic
1/4 cup of finely minced ginger (60mL)

Directions:

- In a glass bowl combine all the ingredients for the barbecue sauce and mix well. Rub over the ribs making sure to coat the ribs evenly. Cover and refrigerate for 30 minutes or up to 4 hours.

- Remove ribs from the fridge 30 minutes prior to cooking them. Place on a baking sheet and reserve the marinade for basting. Allow the meat to come to room temperature.

- Preheat grill to 300F (150C). Just before use, brush the grilling rack with flavored cooking oil.

- Place ribs meaty side up (bone side down) in the center of the rack. Close the lid of the grill and regulate the heat so that it remains at 300F (150C).

- Grill the ribs until the meat begins to shrink away from the ends of the rib bones, approximately 2 hours.

- After 2 hours, begin basting the ribs every 5 minutes for a total of 25 minutes until ribs are done.

- To serve, cut ribs into individual portions.

Serves 4

BOURBON-GLAZED SMOKED SPARERIBS

Slow smoking the ribs with hickory or mesquite adds a taste note on top of the rub and the basting liquid and the sauce. So much love from one pig.

5 slabs of pork spareribs, trimmed of chine bone and brisket flap – 3 lbs (1.5kg) each

3 cups of woodchips (hickory or mesquite)

Dry Rub

1/3 cup freshly ground black pepper (75mL)

1/3 cup paprika (75mL)

2 tbsp brown sugar (30mL)

1 1/2 tsp chili powder (7.5mL)

2 teaspoons garlic powder (10mL)

2 teaspoons onion powder (10mL)

Basting Liquid

3/4 cup of bourbon (188mL)

3/4 cup of cider vinegar (188mL)

1/2 cup of water (125mL)

Directions:

- Combine the rub ingredients in a large bowl. Rub half of the rub mixture into the ribs and reserve the other half of the rub for use the next day. Place the ribs in a large plastic bag and refrigerate overnight.

- A half hour before you plan to put the ribs on the grill, remove them from the plastic bag and apply the remaining rub from the day before. Let the ribs stand for half an hour to come to room temperature. This will ensure that they cook evenly on the grill.

- Place 1 cup of the woodchips in cold water to soak for half an hour.

- If your grill has several grates, remove one on the far side and set it aside. Preheat the grill to high heat – approximately 400–450F (200–225C).

- Squeeze the excess water from the soaking woodchips and place in the center of a large piece of tin foil. Add the remaining 2 cups of dry woodchips. Fold the aluminum foil around the chips to create a sealed pouch. Using a fork, poke holes in the package on both sides to allow the smoke to filter through.

BBQ Sauce

> 1/3 cup of butter (75mL)
>
> 3 medium onions, minced
>
> 1 1/2 cups bourbon (250mL)
>
> 2 tbsp tomato paste (30mL)
>
> 1/3 cup apple cider (75mL)
>
> 1/3 cup orange juice (75mL)
>
> 1/3 cup of pure maple syrup (75mL)
>
> 1 tbsp of dark molasses (15mL)
>
> 1/2 tsp of black pepper

- Place the smoke package directly over the flame on the far side where the grate has been removed. Close the lid and wait for smoke to start building in the barbecue.

- Once smoking has begun lower the heat under the woodchip pouch and turn the heat off on the other portions of the grill. Wait for the temperature to reach approximately 200F (100C).

- Place the ribs on the grates where the heat is off. Close the lid and allow to smoke with indirect heat for approximately 4 hours, turning and mopping with basting liquid at 1 1/2 hours and 3 hours.

- After the ribs have smoked for approximately 3 hours, brush them with the BBQ sauce. Brush them again 20 minutes later.

- Place the remaining sauce in a small pot on the stovetop and reduce for 15 minutes.

- When the ribs are ready to come off the smoker, cover them in foil and allow them to sit for 10–15 minutes to allow the juices to reconstitute. Serve with hot BBQ sauce.

BBQ Sauce

- To prepare the barbecue sauce, melt butter in a saucepan over medium heat. Add the onions and sauté until golden. Add remaining ingredients and lower the heat to low. Let this mixture reduce and thicken for approximately 40 minutes, stirring every 5 minutes.

Serves 10

COUNTRY STYLE RIBS

Remember that the longer you let the ribs sit with the rub on them, the better the taste. The rub is granular and tears little pockets into the flesh when you rub it in. Letting the ribs sit in the fridge overnight allows the flavor to get into the top layer of the meat. A wet marinade on the other hand will soak right through the meat for a more all round flavor profile.

5 lb slab country style pork ribs (2.5kg)

Rib Rub

1 tbsp Spanish paprika (15mL)

3 tbsp brown sugar (45mL)

1 tsp chili powder (5mL)

Directions:

- Place all rub ingredients into a small bowl and stir until well combined. Rub evenly over ribs. Place ribs on a tray, cover with plastic wrap and refrigerate overnight.

2 tsp garlic powder (10mL)

2 tsp onion powder (10mL)

1 tsp fresh thyme (5mL)

2 tsp dry mustard (10mL)

1 tbsp coarse kosher salt (15mL)

Rib Sauce

1 tbsp olive oil (15mL)

1/4 cup chopped onions (60mL)

1 cup chopped canned tomatoes (250mL)

2 tbsp dark molasses (30mL)

1/2 tsp dry mustard (2.5mL)

1/2 tsp chili flakes (2.5mL)

1 tbsp Worcestershire sauce (15mL)

Salt and pepper to taste

- Melt olive oil in a medium sized skillet at high heat. Add onions and sauté for 2-3 minutes or until translucent. Add the remaining ingredients. Reduce heat to medium low and allow sauce to simmer for 15-20 minutes. Remove from heat.

- Remove ribs from fridge and allow to come to room temperature

- Prepare barbecue for indirect heat. Heat one side of the grill to 220F (110C) or low heat and keep the other side of the grill off. Place drip pan under the cool side of the grill.

- Using basting brush, paint the ribs with rib sauce.

- Place the ribs on cool side of the grill over drip pan.

- Slow cook ribs for 3 hours basting with rib sauce every 30 minutes.

Serves 6

DARK-BEER-MARINATED PORK TENDERLOIN

There's more taste going on in a dark beer so don't even think of substituting some light beer stuff. It's all about the yeasty taste soaking into the meat.

6 pork tenderloin, 1 1/2 lb (750g) each

2 bottles (330mL each) dark beer

2 tbsp Dijon mustard (30mL)

2 1/2 tsp horseradish (15mL)

2 tsp black pepper (10mL)

3 sprigs fresh thyme

3 onions, diced

2 tbsp olive oil

Salt to taste

Directions:

- Place the pork in a large, sealable plastic bag. Combine the dark beer, mustard, horseradish, pepper and thyme in a bowl. Mix together and pour into the plastic bag over the pork. Add the onions and seal the bag – removing as much air as possible. Massage the marinade into the meat and ensure that it is well-coated.

- Refrigerate for 5 hours.

- Remove the pork from the bag and pat dry. Strain the marinade into a saucepan and discard the onion. Reduce the marinade on a stove top for approximately 20 minutes, until the sauce coats the back of a spoon.

- Heat the barbecue to medium high 350F (150C). Rub the tenderloin with olive oil and season with salt.

- Place the meat on the grill and sear until golden brown, rotating to ensure char marks are evident all over the meat. Reduce the heat to 275F (135C) and continue to cook the tenderloin, basting with the thickened marinade every 5 minutes for 15–20 minutes. Serve and enjoy!

Serves 6

DRY CARIBBEAN BABY BACK RIBS

Rum mixed with cinnamon, cloves and allspice. Sounds like a Christmas dish, not a barbecue dish. You'll be pleasantly surprised by this shift away from the ordinary.

4 racks of pork baby back ribs

2 cups mesquite woodchips soaked in
    water for 2 hours

1 cup of dried hickory-flavored woodchips

Marinade

2 cups dark rum (500mL)

1 whole star anise

Dry Caribbean Rub

1 tbsp chili powder (15mL)

1 tbsp dried chives (15mL)

1 tbsp dried onion flakes (15mL)

1 tbsp coarse salt (15mL)

1 tsp fresh ginger, chopped (5mL)

1 tsp freshly ground black pepper (5mL)

1 tsp ground allspice (5mL)

1/2 tsp ground star anise (2.5mL)

1/4 tsp ground nutmeg (1.25mL)

Directions:

- Place rib with dark rum and star anise into large sealable plastic bag(s) and marinade for 3 hours in the refrigerator.

- Prepare Dry Caribbean Rub (see below).

- Drain dark rum marinade from ribs and pat dry with paper towel.

- Work rub over ribs and place back into the fridge to finish marinating for at least 1 hour.

- Preheat grill to high.

- Squeeze the soaking chips dry and combine with the dry chips. Place the chip mixture into a double layer of foil. Close the foil around the chips to make a small package. Poke holes in the foil package on both sides and place directly on top of the coals or gas flame. When the package starts smoking, reduce the heat to medium. Arrange ribs onto hot grate, over the drip pan. Cover and let smoke cook for 2 hours or until meat is very tender and has shrunk back from the ends of the bones.

Dry Caribbean Rub:

- Combine chili powder, chives, onion flakes, salt, ginger, black pepper, allspice, star anise and nutmeg and grind using a spice grinder or mortar and pestle, until you have a fine powder.

Serves 4

PROSCIUTTO-WRAPPED FIGS STUFFED WITH BLUE CHEESE

This is a classic summertime starter. Sit around the patio table and gobble up these figs with a nice glass of wine and some good tunes on the stereo. It's a great way to start an evening with friends and family.

12 figs

1/4 lb prosciutto, thinly sliced (113g)

Blue Cheese Stuffing

4 walnuts, chopped fine

1/4 lb of blue cheese (113g)

1 tbsp cognac (15mL)

1 tsp cracked pepper (5mL)

Raspberry Vinegar

1/2 cup frozen defrosted raspberries (125mL)

1 tsp cracked pepper (5mL)

1 tbsp balsamic vinegar (15mL)

Directions:

- Cut into the figs halfway, being careful not to go all the way through. In a small bowl combine stuffing ingredients.

- Stuff the figs with cheese mixture. Wrap prosciutto evenly around figs. If necessary secure with a tooth pick. Place on well-oiled tray.

- In a small bowl combine raspberry vinegar ingredients and reserve.

- Preheat BBQ to medium-high heat 375F (190C). Oil the grill.

- Brush the figs with raspberry vinegar, place on grill and close lid. Cook for 2 minutes, then rotate figs and cook for a further 2 minutes or until prosciutto is crispy and cheese is melted.

- Remove from grill, serve and enjoy!

Serves 12 appetizer portions

GRILLED FRESH-HERB-BRINED PORK CHOPS

This ain't your Mom's dry pork chop (sorry to all Moms out there!). Brining just means soaking the meat in a liquid with some acidic component (in this case it's apple cider and balsamic) that helps "loosen up" the meat and makes it very tender and juicy.

6 bone-in loin pork chops, each about
  1-inch thick

3 tbsp brown sugar (45mL)

1 tbsp kosher salt (15mL)

1 cup apple cider (250mL)

2 cups cold water (500mL)

2 tbsp olive oil (30 mL) plus olive oil
  for grilling

2 tbsp balsamic vinegar (30 mL)

1 tsp freshly ground black pepper (5 mL)

3 whole sprigs fresh rosemary

2 bay leaves

Directions:

- Combine brown sugar, kosher salt and apple cider in a medium bowl. Stir to dissolve.

- Add water, olive oil, balsamic vinegar, pepper, rosemary and bay leaves.

- Put the pork chops into 2 large sealable plastic bags doubled up. The plastic bags can be standing in a large pot to make it more secure. Pour the brine overtop. Seal the plastic bag and put in the refrigerator to rest for 4 hours.

- Remove the pork chops from the brine and place on a large tray. Pat them dry with paper towel and dispose of the brine. Allow the pork chops to come to room temperature before grilling.

- Preheat the barbecue to 475F (240C).

- Lightly brush both sides of the pork chops with olive oil and season with salt and pepper. Sear the pork chops over direct heat for 2 minutes per side, or until golden brown char marks are achieved.

- Lower the temperature to 300F (150C). Turn off one side of barbecue; continue to cook pork chops over indirect heat (the turned-off side of the BBQ), for a further 15 minutes or until desired doneness.

- Once the juices run clear, take the pork chops off the grill and tent with aluminum foil. Allow meat to rest for 10 minutes before serving.

Serves 6

PULLED PORK PICNIC ROAST

This recipe calls for the big marbled fatty picnic pork shoulder roast. After 5 1/2 hours of slow cooking, you're left with an amazing, melt-in-your-mouth roast that goes great with the peach chutney recipe on page 222.

8 lb picnic pork shoulder

Dry Rub

1 cup brown sugar (250mL)

1 tbsp red pepper flakes (15mL)

1 tbsp dry mustard (15mL)

2 tsp garlic powder (10mL)

2 tsp onion powder (10mL)

2 tsp paprika (10mL)

1 tsp marjoram (5mL)

1 tbsp lemon pepper (15mL)

Drip Pan Ingredients

4 sprigs rosemary

1 cup white wine (250mL)

Directions:

- Combine the rub ingredients together in a medium sized bowl. Rub evenly all over pork shoulder. Place pork in a large sealable plastic bag and refrigerate overnight or up to 24 hours.

- Remove the pork from the bag and set it aside so that it may come to room temperature.

- Prepare grill. Place a drip pan underneath the grill grate on one side of the barbecue, add rosemary and wine to drip pan. Preheat the grill using indirect heat by leaving the heat off under the drip pan and putting the far burner on 220F (104C) or medium heat.

- Place pork on cool side of barbecue over drip pan.

- Close lid and let pork grill slowly for 5 1/2 hours.

Serves 12

ROOT BEER RIBS

Hey, why not? We've done cola before, so why not root beer? It's got the sugar
necessary to give the ribs a sweet bite combined with the heat of the chili flakes.

4 sides baby back ribs, approx. 3 lb
  (1.5 kg) each

3 cups cherry woodchips

Marinade

4 cups root beer (1L)

1 cup bourbon (250mL)

1 cup brown sugar (250mL)

2 tbsp dry mustard powder (30mL)

1 1/2 tsp chili flakes (7.5mL)

1 tbsp garlic, finely chopped (15mL)

3 sprigs of fresh rosemary, bruised

Directions:

- Combine marinade ingredients in a medium bowl.

- Place ribs in a non-reactive (glass or ceramic) dish.
  Pour marinade over ribs and cover with plastic.
  Refrigerate for 4 hours.

- Place 2 cups of the woodchips in cold water to
  soak for 1/2 hour.

- If your grill has several grates, remove one on the
  far side and set it aside. Preheat 350F (176C) or
  medium heat.

- Squeeze the excess water from the soaking woodchips and place in the center of a large piece of tin foil. Add the remaining 1 cup of dry woodchips. Fold the aluminum foil around the chips to create a sealed pouch. Using a fork, poke holes in the package on both sides to allow the smoke to filter through.

- Place the smoke package directly over the flame on the far side where the grate has been removed. Close the lid and wait for smoke to start building in the barbecue.

- Once smoking has begun, lower the heat under the woodchip pouch and turn the heat off on the other portions of the grill. Wait for the temperature to reach approximately 275F (135C).

- Place ribs over the cool side of the grill. Close lid and smoke for 3 hours or until meat is falling off the bone.

- Remove from barbecue and loosely tent ribs with foil. Let ribs rest for 10 minutes before serving.

Serves 12

RUBBED SMOKED PORK TENDERLOIN CAJUN-STYLE

Dried herbs can be substituted if fresh are unavailable. Note: use about 1/3 less dried herb than the recipe calls for, since the flavor of dried herbs is more intense. To retain that beautiful crust on the outside of your meat, place cooked meat on a wire rack with a dish under it while letting rest (or tent). Use the juices if you'd like. No need to waste them!

2 pork tenderloins, thin sliver skin removed

3 cups cherry woodchips (750mL)

Directions:

- Combine the rub ingredients in a small bowl.

- Rub mixture vigorously over pork, coating the meat. Place pork in a large sealable plastic bag and refrigerate for 3 hours. Remove from fridge a half hour before smoking to bring to room temperature.

Dry Rub

1/2 cup coarse salt (kosher or sea) (60mL)

4 tbsp sweet paprika (60mL)

3 tbsp garlic powder (45mL)

3 tbsp onion powder (45mL)

2 tbsp fresh thyme, chopped (30mL)

2 tbsp fresh oregano, chopped (30mL)

1 tbsp freshly ground black pepper (15mL)

2 tsp fresh sage leaves (10mL)

1 tsp cayenne pepper (5mL)

Watercress and Parmesan Cheese Salad

1 bunch watercress, washed and dried

1 cup parmesan cheese shavings (250mL)

1/2 cup sundried cranberries (125mL)

Dressing

Juice of 2 lemons

Salt and pepper to taste

1/4 cup olive oil (60mL)

- Soak 2 cups (500mL) of cherry woodchips in water for 1 hour.

- Squeeze the excess water from the woodchips and place in the center of a large piece of foil. Add 1 cup (250mL) of dry woodchips and mix. Close the foil around the chips sealing the package. Using a fork, poke holes in both sides of the package.

- Prepare the barbecue for smoking. Preheat one side of the barbecue to 400F (200C) or to high heat. Leave the other side off. Place the smoke pouch underneath the grill directly over high-heat source of the grill. Close the lid and wait for smoke.

- Once barbecue cavity is full of smoke, place tenderloin on the cool side of the grill. Turn the temperature down to 220F (104C) or medium-low.

- Smoke pork for 45 minutes. Remove from grill and loosely tent with foil. Allow meat to rest for 10 minutes before slicing.

- Slice tenderloin against the grain of the meat and serve with the Watercress and Parmesan Cheese salad (recipe follows).

Watercress and Parmesan Cheese Salad

- In a medium sized bowl, whisk together lemon juice and olive oil. Add salt and pepper to taste.

- Spread arugula on a platter and arrange sliced pork tenderloin on top. Sprinkle with parmesan shavings and cranberries.

- Pour dressing over salad. Toss gently to combine.

SLOW-SMOKED THAI RIBS

You can buy fish sauce in pretty much any grocery store these days. On the other hand, it's worth the trip down to your local Chinatown for a big bottle of the stuff at half the price of the "anglosized" version in the Big Box store. Plus Chinatown is a very cool place to hang out.

3 x 1 1/2 lb racks of baby back ribs,
  membrane removed
3 cups apple woodchips (750mL)

Directions:

- In a large bowl whisk together Thai marinade ingredients, set aside.

- Place ribs in a sealable plastic bag. Pour marinade over ribs and place in the refrigerator. Let marinate for 4 hours.

Thai Marinade

2 tbsp peanut oil (30mL)

2 tsp of sesame oil (10mL)

2 tbsp fish sauce (30mL)

2 tbsp garlic, minced (30mL)

1 tbsp fresh ginger, minced (15mL)

1/4 cup chopped fresh cilantro (60mL)

2 stalks lemongrass, outer leaves removed
    and center thinly sliced

2 tbsp sugar (30mL)

1 tbsp of rice wine vinegar (15mL)

Juice of 2 limes

Dipping and Basting Sauce

1 tbsp rice wine vinegar (15mL)

1/2 cup pineapple juice (125mL)

Juice of 2 limes

2 tbsp white sugar (30mL)

1 tbsp garlic, chopped (15mL)

1 tsp chili pure (10mL)

1 stalk lemongrass, finely chopped

- In a small bowl, whisk together dipping and basting sauce and set aside. Cover with plastic wrap and refrigerate until time to baste the ribs.

- Soak only 2 cups (500mL) of the apple woodchips in water for 1 hour.

- Prepare barbecue for grilling with indirect heat by preheating one side of the grill to 400F (200C) or high heat and leaving the other side of the grill off.

- Prepare a smoke pouch by squeezing the excess liquid from the soaked woodchips and place them on the center of a large piece of tin foil. Combine the dry woodchips with the wet and fold the foil around the woodchips creating a pouch. Using a fork, poke several holes in the smoke pouch and place it under the grate on the heated side of the barbecue. Close the lid and wait for smoke.

- Once you have smoke, lower the heat under the smoke pouch to 275F (135C) or medium heat and place the ribs on the opposite side of the grill where the burner remains off.

- Close the lid and smoke ribs for 2 1/2 hours. Baste ribs with dipping and basting sauce in the last half hour. Serve with remaining sauce.

Serves 6

SMOKEY CANADIAN BACON

How did back bacon ever become a Canadian icon? Was it just Bob and Doug? Nah. Anyway, here's a really simple way of smoking your own back bacon, which you can then use in tons of different dishes.

2 lb (1kg) Canadian bacon (back bacon)

4 tbsp vegetable oil (60mL)

4 tbsp brown sugar (60mL)

1 tbsp coarse or kosher salt (15mL)

1 1/2 tsp cayenne pepper (15mL)

2 tbsp ground cinnamon (30mL)

2 tbsp fresh ground black pepper (30mL)

*2 cups apple woodchips, soaked and
    ready for smoking*

2 cups of dry apple woodchips

Directions:

- Rub the Canadian bacon with the vegetable oil.

- Combine all the other ingredients in a bowl and mix them together well. Spread the rub over the bacon, ensuring it is evenly coated. Wrap the meat in plastic and refrigerate for 2 hours.

- Remove the bacon from the fridge and allow it to come to room temperature.

- Prepare the grill for smoking at 200–220F (100C–110C). Squeeze the soaking chips dry and combine with the dry chips. Place the chip mixture into a double layer of foil. Close the foil around the chips to make a small package. Poke holes in the foil package on both sides and place directly on top of the coals or gas flame. It will take approximately 15 minutes for the chips to begin smoking.

- Once the chips begin to smoke, place the bacon on the grill and close the lid. Leave to cook slowly for 90 minutes. Flip the bacon once halfway through the cooking process.

- Let the bacon rest for 20 minutes under some foil to keep the juices in, before slicing and serving.

Serves 8

STUFFED PORK TENDERLOIN WITH GOLDEN RAISIN GLAZE

Pork with something sweet and sour on it is sheer perfection. Much like turkey with cranberry sauce. It's a natural! Tenderloin is a very lean cut of meat so don't overcook, or it'll be tough and dry as shoe leather (not that I've eaten shoe leather!).

3 pork tenderloins, 12 oz (350g) each

10 oz cream cheese (300g)

Zest of 2 limes

2 tbsp fresh sage, roughly chopped (30mL)

Salt and pepper to taste

1 cup spinach leaves washed and dried (250mL)

3 tbsp olive oil (45mL)

3 cups fruitwood chips (apple wood or cherry wood) (750mL)

Glaze

1 cup golden raisins soaked in 1/2 cup port wine

1/2 cup red wine (125mL).

1 tsp cracked black pepper (5mL)

1 tbsp fresh mint leaves (15mL)

1 tbsp lemon juice (15mL)

Directions:

- In a medium bowl mix together cream cheese, lime zest, sage, salt and pepper.

- Using a sharp knife, carefully open the tenderloin like a book by making a slit down the length of the meat without going all the way through the other side. Lay the meat between two sheets of parchment paper and pound with a rolling pin or meat tenderizer to an even thickness of about 1/2 inch (1 cm). Lift off the parchment paper and drizzle the meat with olive oil. Lightly season the pork with pepper. Lay spinach leaves down evenly over pork. Crumble cream cheese mixture over the spinach. Roll the pork up lengthways to form a large sausage-shaped roll and tie with butcher twine. Place on a baking tray and drizzle with oil. Cover with plastic wrap and refrigerate until ready to cook.

- Place 2 cups (500mL) of the woodchips in water to soak for 1 hour.

- To prepare glaze, warm the wine and soaked raisins in a medium saucepan over medium heat, add pepper and let cook for 5 minutes. Remove pan from heat and add the lemon juice and mint. Set aside as basting for pork.

- Prepare barbecue for grilling by preheating one side of the grill to 400F (200C) or high heat and the other side of the grill to 375F (190C) or medium-high heat.

- Drain wet chips from water and squeeze out excess liquid. Place on a large sheet of foil, add dry woodchips and wrap loosely to form a pouch. Using a fork, poke holes on both sides of the pouch. Remove the grill grate from the barbecue and place the smoke pouch directly on the high heat source. Oil the grill.

- Place tenderloin over medium heat side and cook for 3 minutes or until char marks are achieved. Flip the pork and cook for another 3 minutes. Turn the heat source directly under pork off.

- Using a pastry brush, glaze the tenderloins with golden raisin mixture.

- When smoke starts to billow out of the barbecue turn the heat source under smoke pouch to 325F (162C) or medium heat.

- Let pork smoke for 15 minutes and then glaze again. Let cook for 10 more minutes and remove. Place on tray and loosely tent with foil. Let meat rest 10 minutes before slicing.

Serves 6–8

"TO LIVE FOR" PANCETTA AND POTATO PACKAGE

We call this one "to live for" because once you've tasted it, you'll want to live forever just to keep eating it once every couple of weeks or so.

6 large new potatoes, sliced into disks

2 white leeks, chopped 1/4-inch thick

3 cloves garlic, sliced

10 fresh sage leaves

10 thick slices pancetta, cooked

3 oz gorgonzola cheese

1/2 cup cream (125mL)

Salt and pepper to taste

Directions:

* Preheat barbecue to 325F (162C) or medium heat.

* Tear off a large piece of foil (enough to make an 8 x 8 package), place 1/3 of the potatoes on foil and season with salt and pepper.

* Top with 1/2 of the leeks, pancetta, garlic and sage.

* Place another layer of potatoes on top of the mixture. Top that layer with the remaining leeks, pancetta, garlic and sage and season with pepper. Top with the last of the potatoes.

* Fold up sides of foil package. Sprinkle the layers with gorgonzola and add cream.

* Seal the foil package.

* Place package on grill. Cook for 30 minutes or until potatoes are tender.

Serves 6

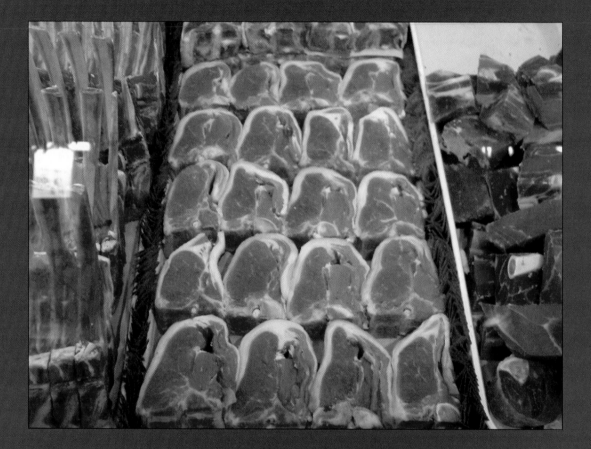

Feeling A Little Sheepish

Mary had a little lamb
Its fleece was white as snow
And everywhere that Mary went
The lamb was sure to go.
–MRS. SARAH JOSEPHA (BUELL) HALE, 1830

Apple Wood-Smoked Lamb Shoulder

Buffalo Burgers

Gin-Smoked Lamb

Grilled Lamb Chops

Grilled Venison Chops

Lamb Burgers

Lamb Kabobs

Pecan and Honey-Crusted Rack of Lamb

Roasted Leg of Lamb

Spicy Lamb Ribs

Stuffed Leg of Lamb

Lamb and game meats are not just for exotic tastes. They are becoming increasingly popular on restaurant menus and can be ordered from most butcher shops. Adding lamb and game to your grilling repertoire will awaken the taste buds.

Game animals, like lamb, venison and buffalo, are so named because they have been traditionally hunted for sport and these meats are thus described as having a "gamey" flavor and texture. I would describe the taste as stronger than beef, and slightly chewier, too – more so if cooked incorrectly. That mysterious, gamey flavor is a result of the combinations of foods the animal eats in the wild: everything from berries to leaves and grasses (and really, who knows what else?). Since all commercially-raised animals eat what we give them, the industry regulates exactly how the resulting meat will taste.

The recipes in this section are primarily for lamb, with one each for venison (deer meat) and buffalo, as these are becoming increasingly available and more popular than ever.

BAAAHHH!

In North America, lamb has always lagged behind beef, pork and chicken in consumption levels. North Americans eat about 0.7 pounds of lamb per person per year as opposed to New Zealanders who consume approximately 56.5 pounds. That's a huge difference! The two factors contributing to that difference are lack of availability and tradition. The west was won on the back of a horse after all – driving cattle, not sheep. There is a long and deep-rooted association with beef in North America. However, our interest in new cultures – particularly their cuisine – coupled with increasing immigration, the diverse range of ethnic cookbooks now available, and the proliferation of global media has introduced us to new foods and traditions – the enjoyment of lamb being one.

New Zealand, Australia and the Middle East are all major producers and consumers of lamb and mutton. People arriving in North America from these parts of the world bring not only their hopes and dreams, but also their favorite recipes, which are ingrained in their culture. Since these recipes require specialized ingredients, the North American marketplace in turn adapts.

Anatomy 101

Lamb is bred on virtually every continent, including ours. Naturally, I have a few favorite breeds. New Zealand and Australian lamb are great if you're serving to lamb enthusiasts. They tend toward a bold flavor and can be a bit chewy – delicious when properly prepared. Canadian lamb (particularly from Alberta) and Washington State lamb are at the top of my list because they taste less gamey. If you're serving to a diverse group of people, this will surely be a great middle ground. I find that folks new to lamb don't take to it if it's too "wild/gamey" tasting. The Canadian and Washington State lamb have a mild flavor and are forgiving in many different recipes. The texture tends to be silkier and it can be quite tender, much like beef.

A lamb is processed for consumption between the ages of 6–12 months. The smaller, younger animals are usually more tender and mild-flavored than the bigger, older animals. If a lamb is older than 12 months it must be labeled "mutton." The only way to tell the age of the cut is by comparing sizes of the whole legs. Legs 9 pounds and up are older than legs 6 pounds or under. But don't avoid the older cuts altogether. Low-and-slow is a must here. With care, your mutton will be tender and very flavorful!

By now you're familiar with primal cuts of meat. Lamb is similar to beef and pork, however, there are 5 primal cuts for lamb to beef's 8 and pork's 4:

Shoulder: From the neck to the fourth rib. This meat is flavorful, but it contains a lot of connective tissues. Roasts, boneless stewing meat, ground meat and chops come from here. Low-and-slow works best. I love to cook ground lamb with a bit of onion and light seasonings. Put it on a pita with some lettuce, tomato and baba ganoush or tahini and you've got a definite crowd pleaser!

Rib: The rib area sits right behind the shoulder toward the back of the animal. It encompasses the 5th–12th ribs. All eight sections of the ribs together are called the "rack." I like to sprinkle it with salt and pepper and sear it, which caramelizes the exterior. Then I put some Dijon mustard on it, role it in breadcrumbs and spices and cook it bone-side down on indirect heat until it is medium-rare at 125F. The ribs can also be separated and eaten as lamb chops. This meat has a mild flavor and tender texture, is perfect for a marinade, and is quite frankly my favorite. Lamb chops have two types of meat, the strip loin and the tenderloin, which come from the part of the animal that doesn't get a lot of movement, making the meat very tender.

Loin: The loin area starts at the last rib and includes the hip. The loin chop, sometimes called the lamb T-bone, is a popular cut because of its extremely tender and mild – almost sweet – flavor. However, it does tend to be a bit pricy. Sear it, turn the heat down and remove just before it's perfectly cooked – tent for 10 minutes – sheer perfection! Or should I say, "sheep perfection"?

Leg: From the hip to the hoof, the leg is either sold whole or cut up into roasts and shanks, with bones in or out. I personally like to cook leg meat with the bone in, as I feel it imparts more flavor to the meat. I'll also use the leg meat for kebabs, which is a family favorite.

Foreshank and Breast: This area includes the front legs. Each produces a shank and the underbelly, which houses a breast. The foreshank is the leanest cut on the lamb and requires low-and-slow cooking. The breast is often boned, rolled and stuffed and cooked using a moist heat.

Oh Give Me A Home

Where do the buffalo roam these days? Buffalo (also commonly referred to as "bison"), once the main food source for the Plains Indians, used to number in the tens of millions until they were slaughtered indiscriminately. By 1900 there were approximately only 13 American buffalo left, all of them in Yellowstone Park. Today, buffalo farming is a growing industry. There are now 300,000 bison roaming the countryside and out of that, 280,000 are farmed on private ranches.

I'm not going to spend too much time on buffalo meat, however I do want to help spread the word. Buffalo has a rich red meat that is extremely low in fat and high in iron. It's lower in cholesterol than beef, chicken and most fish! A 3-ounce serving of bison contains only 93 calories, 1.8 grams of fat and 43 milligrams of cholesterol. That's music to my doctor's ears!

Farm-raised buffalo are grown without the use of antibiotics or steroids and are allowed to roam (just like in the song). Because the animal eats fresh grass, the meat tends to have a rich, almost beefy taste – not pungent or gamey like some breeds of lamb. Since it is virtually fat-free, cooks should be mindful of the need to keep moisture in the meat. If you're grilling a steak, give it a quick sear, then low indirect heat until medium-rare – it's wonderful. Approximate cooking times:

1-inch thick: Rare 6-8 minutes. Medium 10-12 minutes
11/2-inch thick: Rare 10-12 minutes. Medium14-18 Minutes
2-inch thick: Rare 14-20 minutes. Medium: 20-25 Minutes

For a roast, sear then switch to low-and-slow. Keep a very close eye on the internal temperature:

Doneness:	Internal Temperature:
Rare	130-135 F (54-57C)
Medium-rare	135-140 F (57-60C)
Medium	140-145 F (60-63C)
Medium-well	150-155 F (65.5-68C)
Well-done	155-160 F (68-71C)

Remember, there is very little fat in this meat! Do not overcook it. By the way, tenting is going to work wonders here. Remove from heat just before cooked and cover (tent) for 10 minutes. I've included one buffalo meat recipe in this section for you to try. Once you've mastered that, put your own special touch on it.

Venison is Good Medicine

Venison is much like buffalo meat in composition and nutritional value. It's lean, as low as 0.2% fat for a 4-ounce serving of steak, with 22.9% protein and 0.2% fiber. Because of its leanness, steaks take well to a quick searing to medium rare. Venison can be compared to beef, both in texture and flavor. Roasts do well with the low-and-slow method. The same cooking guidelines for bison meat apply to venison.

It is believed that reindeer were the first domesticated deer. A letter written by Norway's King Ottar in the ninth century describes his fine herd of 600 reindeer. Deer farms have been documented as far back as 2000 BC in China and venison was once a staple food for much of the world. Today deer farming is on the rise as our health-conscious society is beginning to see its benefits.

Let your taste buds do some exploring and discover meats from different cultures and eras. If properly prepared, you won't be disappointed!

Look what venison does to a goofy guitar player from Detroit! I'm going to be 54 this year and if I had any more energy I'd scare you.
–TED NUGENT, ROCK STAR AND HUNTING ACTIVIST

APPLE WOOD-SMOKED LAMB SHOULDER

You're going to cook this one for six hours. That's right, a whole day of barbecueing for the most amazingly tender lamb roast you've ever had. When you're finished cooking, let the lamb sit under tented tin foil for at least half an hour. To juice onion, pulse in blender to a purée, then strain juice through cheese cloth.

6 lb (3kg) lamb shoulder, bone-in

6 cups apple woodchips, soaked in water
*   for 2 hours*
3 cups dry apple woodchips

Marinade

3 tbsp light soya sauce (45mL)

1/2 cup of white onion, juiced (125mL)

2 tbsp ginger (30mL)

1 tbsp garlic (15mL)

2 tbsp red wine vinegar (30mL)

2 tsp Five Spice Powder (10mL) (page 74)

1 tbsp honey (15mL)

1/4 cup olive oil (60mL)

1 cup beer (250mL)

Pita bread and yogurt (optional)

Directions:

- To juice onion, pulse in blender to a puree, then strain juice through cheese cloth

- Prepare marinade by combining all ingredients in a medium-sized bowl.

- Place lamb in a large, sealable plastic bag or non-reactive bowl and pour marinade over top; ensure the entire surface of the lamb is coated.

- Refrigerate for a minimum of 5 hours or overnight. Remove from fridge 1/2 hour before you plan to start barbecuing.

- You will need a total of three smoke pouches. To build a smoke pouch, drain 2 cups (500mL) of the wet woodchips and squeeze excess water out. Spread wet woodchips on a large piece of aluminum foil. Place 1 cup (250mL) of dry wood-chips on top and mix them together. Close foil around chips to make a sealed foil package. Using a fork, puncture holes on the top and bottom of pack.

- Place the smoke pouch under the grate on one side of the grill. Turn heat under the smoke pouch to 400F (200C) or high heat, and close lid. Wait for smoke. Once you see smoke starting to billow out of the barbecue, lower heat under the smoke pouch to 200F (100C) or low heat.

- Place lamb on cool side of the grill. Close the lid and cook for 1 hour per pound of lamb.

- Change smoke pouch every hour and a half.

Serves 6

BUFFALO BURGERS

Remember, buffalo meat is very lean and tasty! In this preparation, you'll be hard pressed to tell it apart from beef. Give it a try. I think you'll be pleasantly surprised!

2 lb lean ground buffalo meat (1kg)

1/2 cup butter, softened (125mL)

1 green onion, finely chopped

2 tbsp cilantro, chopped (30mL)

2 tbsp parsley, chopped (30mL)

1 small, red hot thai chili pepper,
   finely minced

Salt and pepper to taste

Directions:

- In a medium bowl, combine butter, green onion, cilantro, parsley and hot red pepper.

- On a piece of plastic wrap or waxed paper, form the butter mixture into a cylinder, about 1 inch (1.5 cm) in diameter. Wrap and close the ends. Place the butter cylinder in the freezer to solidify.

- Shape ground buffalo into 6 large balls. Cut frozen butter into six 1/4-inch (4mm) discs.

- Freeze remaining butter for use another day.

- Make a depression in the center of each buffalo meatball. Place a frozen butter disc into each meatball and seal inside. Shape meat into patties about 1-inch (1.5 cm) thick, keeping the butter well surrounded by buffalo meat.

- Preheat the barbecue to 375F (190C) or medium-high heat.

- Oil the grill and season the buffalo burgers with salt and pepper.

- Grill the burgers 6 minutes per side.

Serves 6

GIN-SMOKED LAMB

Gin has flavors of juniper berry and berries go really well with lamb. Try pouring a little extra gin into a tall glass with lots of ice and a twist of lemon to sip on while the lamb is cooking.

1 medium-sized onion, chopped

2 cloves garlic

2 lemons, juiced

5 tbsp gin (75mL)

2 tbsp kosher salt (30mL)

1/4 cup olive oil (60mL)

1 x 5 lb leg of lamb (2.5kg)

2 cups cherry woodchips – soaked in
   cold water for 1/2 hour

5 cups dry cherry woodchips

Directions:

- In a food processor combine onion, garlic, lemon, gin and salt and process to combine. Add oil in a thin stream, to form marinade.

- Place leg of lamb into a large sealable plastic bag and add gin marinade. Seal and turn bag to coat the lamb evenly. Refrigerate over night.

- Preheat barbecue to a high heat.

- Drain wet cherry woodchips and combine with dry. Wrap combined woodchips in aluminum foil. Use a fork to puncture holes in the top and bottom of the foil package to allow the smoke to flow through the package. The smoke flavor will infuse the meat.

- Place wood chip package directly over heat until the package begins to smoke. Once smoke is visible, turn to a medium-low heat. (428F /220C).

- Remove marinaded lamb from refrigerator and bring to room temperature.

- Transfer lamb to barbecue and smoke for 35 to 40 minutes per pound or until the internal temperature reads 293F (145C), rare to medium rare.

- Remove the lamb from barbecue and let stand for 10 minutes, slice and serve warm or cold. Enjoy!

Serves 8

GRILLED LAMB CHOPS

There is nothing better on the barbecue than a nice juicy lamb chop; charred on the outside and medium rare on the inside. I like to squeeze a splash of fresh lemon juice on the chops right after they come off the grill.

10 1/2-inch thick lamb chops

Marinade
Juice of 1 ripe beefsteak tomato
1 tbsp garlic, chopped (15mL)
1 tbsp fresh ginger, chopped (15mL)
1/4 cup cilantro, chopped (60mL)
1/4 cup apple cider (60mL)
1 tsp dry mustard (5mL)
3 tbsp brown sugar (30mL)
1/2 cup olive oil (125mL)

Directions:

- Place lamb chops in large, sealable plastic bag.

- Combine marinade ingredients in medium bowl. Mix well and pour over lamb chops. Refrigerate for 6 hours.

- Remove lamb chops from marinade and pat dry. Discard any leftover marinade.

- Preheat barbecue to 325F (190C) or medium heat.

- Drizzle lamb chops with oil and season to taste with salt and pepper.

- Oil barbecue grill and place lamb chops on it. Allow to cook 4 minutes per side (for medium rare) or until desired doneness.

- Remove lamb chops from heat and cover with foil and allow to rest for 5 minutes before slicing.

Serves 10

GRILLED VENISON CHOPS

Venison is very lean and not inexpensive, so please do not overcook. Venison is best served medium rare. Cook it to more than medium and you might as well be grilling soggy old newspaper.

4 racks of venison

Dry Rub

2 tbsp fresh thyme, chopped

2 tbsp fresh rosemary, chopeed

4 tsp of 5 peppercorn mix (10mL)

1 tsp oregano (5mL)

1 tbsp salt (15mL)

Directions:

- Pulse peppercorn in a coffee or spice grinder, add chopped herbs and then rub all over meat. Cover venison and refrigerate for 1–2 hours.

- Preheat one side of barbecue to 375F (190C) or medium-high heat and the other side of barbecue to 250F (120C) or low heat.

- Sear venison 2–3 minutes on each side over the medium-high heat to achieve a crust.

- Move venison over to low side of barbecue and continue to cook for 10–12 minutes for medium rare.

Serves 8

LAMB BURGERS

Any good butcher will have ground lamb on hand. As always, you're encouraged to experiment with ingredients.

1 lb lean ground lamb (500g)

1 tbsp dried mustard powder (15mL)

3 shallots, finely chopped

1 garlic clove, finely chopped

1 tbsp cinnamon (15mL)

1/2 tbsp allspice (7.5mL)

1/2 tbsp coriander (7.5mL)

Salt to taste

1 large egg, beaten

1/4 cup bread crumbs (60mL)

1/3 cup pine nuts, optional (75mL)

Directions:

- Preheat grill to 375F (190C) or medium-high heat.

- Combine all ingredients in a bowl. With cold-water-dampened hands, shape into 4 2-inch thick patties. Place on tray. Cover and refrigerate until ready to grill.

- Lightly oil the grate and grill each burger for 6 minutes per side, or until entirely cooked through. Serve as a sandwich in a pita, or on a burger bun, garnishing if desired with tomato, onion, lettuce and yogurt.

Serves 4

LAMB KABOBS

These are so delicious. No need for a mint sauce with this combo of spices! To ensure evenly cooked meat, cut lamb into 1-inch pieces. Then cut up the center to the middle. Skewer the pieces at the thinner ends and thread.

2-3 lbs (1–1.5kg) boneless leg or shoulder
   of lamb, cut into 1-inch cubes

4 Bermuda onions, cut into big chunks

4 red peppers, cut into squares

2 tbsp parsley, chopped (30 mL)

1 tbsp mint, chopped (15mL)

1 1/2 tsp paprika (7.5mL)

2 tbsp fresh sage, chopped

1/2 tsp freshly ground pepper

5 cloves garlic, finely diced

1/2 tsp salt (2.5mL)

2 tbsp olive oil (30mL)

Bamboo skewers soaked in water

Directions:

- Combine all the ingredients except the lamb, red onions and peppers into a large non-reactive (glass or ceramic) bowl. Mix well. Add the cubes of lamb to the bowl and toss until each piece is well coated. Cover bowl with plastic wrap and refrigerate for 4–8 hours.

- Place some bamboo skewers into water to soak for a minimum of 20 minutes.

- Preheat the grill to medium high heat. If you can't hold your hand over the heat for a count of "5 steamboats" the grill is too hot. Lower the heat and let it cool a bit.

- Arrange the lamb on the skewers alternating with a piece of onion and red pepper between each cube of meat.

- Oil the grill to avoid sticking. Arrange the skewers on the grill so that the tips are off the heat. Let cook for approximately 2–3 minutes per side until nicely browned.

Serves 8

PECAN AND HONEY-CRUSTED RACK OF LAMB

The longer you let the lamb sit in the fridge with the crust on, the better. In the restaurant business, this is known as letting the meat "set up", so that the crust can properly adhere to the lamb. This makes for a better crust when it hits the grill. Be sure to trim the rack of any silver skin or excess fat beforehand. Silver skin is a tough membrane that sometimes is found running across tenderloin meats. If you don't trim it off, it will shrink while cooking and tighten the meat up.

4 racks of lamb, 5 bones each

1 1/2 cups pecans, chopped (375mL)

1/2 cup honey (125mL)

2 tbsp olive oil (30mL)

Zest of 2 limes

1 tbsp cracked black pepper (15mL)

Salt to taste

Directions:

- Season lamb racks with salt and pepper.

- Blend nuts, lime zest, olive oil and honey to form crust.

- Pat crust evenly on racks, pressing down lightly.

- Wrap in plastic wrap and refrigerate for 6 hours or overnight.

- Preheat one side of the barbecue to 375F (190C). Oil barbecue grill rack.

- Place the lamb over the cool side of the grill and cook with the lid down for 15 minutes (for medium rare).

- Remove lamb and loosely cover with foil. Let lamb rest for 10 minutes before carving.

Serves 6

ROASTED LEG OF LAMB

Mint and garlic were made for lamb. This recipe is a simple classic that really takes no time to prepare—with amazing results.

5 lb leg of lamb, butterflyed (2.5 kg)

Stuffing

1/2 bunch of flat leaf parsley, about 20 stems

1/2 bunch mint, about 20 stems

4 garlic cloves

2 tbsp balsamic vinegar (15mL)

Salt and pepper to taste

Directions:

- Blend parsley, mint, garlic and balsamic vinegar in a food processor or blender, pulse to a smooth paste.

- Place leg of lamb skin side down. With a sharp knife cut 1/2 inch (8mm) deep slits across the lamb about 2 inches (5cm) apart.

- Using your fingers push the paste deep into the slits.

- Place on a tray and season with pepper to taste. You may season with a small amount of salt if desired.

- Preheat barbecue to 325° F/162°C or medium heat. Oil the grill.

- Place lamb on grill and cook for 12-15 minutes per side or until crispy dark char-marks are achieved.

- Flip the roast over and continue to cook for another 10–12 minutes. Remove roast from grill, place on tray and loosely cover with foil. Let meat rest 15 minutes before slicing.

Serves 6

SPICY LAMB RIBS

Lamb ribs are tiny compared to what you're normally used to. The meat is tender and they work well with this spicy dipping sauce. Plus, there's no cutlery to wash after dinner.

4–5 pounds lamb ribs (1.8–2.2 kg)

2 dried chipotle peppers, stems removed

2 tsp red chili flakes (10mL)

2 tbsp cumin seed (30mL)

2 tbsp black peppercorns (30mL)

Salt to taste

3 tbsp sugar (45mL)

Olive oil for drizzling

4 cups cherry woodchips (1 litre)

Directions:

- Soak 2 cups of woodchips (500mL) in water for 1 hour. Drain chips and mix with 1 cup of the dry chips (250mL). On a large piece of aluminum foil place the chips and wrap up to form a secure but loose package. Using a fork poke holes through the aluminum foil, this will allow smoke to escape.

- Remove the skin from outer backside of ribs using kitchen pliers.

Barbecue Sauce

2 tbsp minced garlic (30mL)

1 jalapeno pepper seeded and diced

2 chipotle peppers, diced

1 Spanish onion, peeled and chopped

*1 cup of canned, chopped plum tomatoes
    (250mL)*

3 tbsp brown sugar (45mL)

1/4 cup red wine vinegar (60mL)

1/4 cup fresh chopped cilantro (60mL)

2 tbsp olive oil (30mL)

Salt and pepper to taste

Additional chili flakes to taste

- In a spice grinder, grind the chipotle pepper, chili flakes, cumin seeds and peppercorns. Transfer to a medium bowl and add the salt and sugar. Using rubber gloves to keep the hot peppers off your skin, rub the ingredients into the flesh of the lamb tearing the micro fibers of the flesh as you rub.

- Prepare barbecue sauce. In a large sauté pan add olive oil, garlic, onions and peppers and cook until slightly translucent. Add the brown sugar, red wine vinegar and tomatoes. Simmer for 15 minutes. Remove from heat add the cilantro, salt and pepper to taste and chilies, if desired.

- Prepare barbecue for smoking with indirect heat. Remove the grill rack from one side of the barbecue. Place smoke pouch in and turn the heat to high. Close the lid of the barbecue. Once the cavity of the BBQ is full of smoke, place your ribs on the grill rack without direct heat. Reduce heat to 220F (104C) or low temperature and close lid. Smoke ribs for 45 minutes.

- After 45 minutes remove smoke pouch.

- Wrap ribs in foil and return to barbecue. Continue to cook for 2 hours or until meat is almost falling off the bone.

- When ribs are tender remove from heat and baste with sauce. Cover with foil and let rest 10 minutes before carving.

Serves 8

STUFFED LEG OF LAMB

You absolutely have to marinate this leg for 24 hours to get maximum flavor infused into the lamb meat from the white wine and rosemary. And check out the ingredients in the stuffing. Try this once and it will become part of your regular repertoire.

5 to 5 1/2 pounds boned leg of lamb (2.5kg)

1 cup white wine (250mL)

3 sprigs rosemary

Marinade

10 garlic cloves

Juice and zest of one lime

2 tbsp honey (30mL)

1 1/2 tbsp olive oil (22mL)

2 tsp dried rosemary

Stuffing

1 tbsp olive oil (15mL)

2 garlic cloves, sliced in half

1/2 medium onion, chopped

*2 cooked chicken breasts, minced in
    food processor*

*1 1/2 lb spinach, cooked, drained and
    chopped (750g)*

8 oz mild goat cheese (250g)

1/3 cup chopped chives (75mL)

1/4 cup dried cherries (60mL)

1 tsp Worcestershire sauce (5mL)

Salt and pepper to taste

Directions:

- To prepare the marinade, add garlic, honey and the lime zest and juice to a mini food processor. Start the processor and gradually add oil to the mixture until thick and emulsified.

- Place the lamb in a large sealable bag and pour the marinade over top. Shake bag so the meat is thoroughly coated. Place the meat in the refrigerator and marinate overnight, or up to 24 hours.

- Remove the leg of lamb from the marinade and pat dry. Slice 4 slits through the leg and stuff one garlic slice into each. Season the cavity with salt and pepper.

- Stuff the leg of lamb with the stuffing (preparation directions below) and close the meat around the filling. Secure the roast with butcher's twine.

- To prepare lamb for grilling, place in a skillet with hot oil and sear the meat 1–2 minutes on each side.

- Pour wine in drip pan and add rosemary.

- Remove the grill from one side of the barbecue and insert drip pan. Replace grill. Preheat the other side of the grill to 220F (104C).

- Place lamb on grill above the drip pan and cook for 30 minutes per pound. Replenish wine in drip pan as necessary.

Serves 6

Two If By Sea

One fish, Two fish, Red fish, Blue fish
–DR. SEUSS

Blackened Scallops with Guacamole on Tortilla Chips

Cedar-Planked Salmon

Corn Husk Grilled Red Snapper

Crab Legs with Lemon Lime Butter

"Fun Time" Shrimp Quesadillas with Pineapple and Red & Yellow Peppers

Gin-Marinated Grilled Shrimp

Grilled Chipotle-Lime Shrimp

Grilled Clams with Lemon Butter Sauce

Grilled Fresh Sardines

Grilled Lobster with Saffron-Lime Mayonnaise

Grilled Marlin with Coconut Chili Crust

Iced Oysters Off the Grill

Oriental Grilled Catfish

Scallop and Salmon Skewers

Skewered Scallops with Prosciutto

Smoked Prosciutto-Wrapped Cheesy Shrimp

West Indian Rum Shrimp

Wild Salmon with Raspberry Glaze

Seafood, mysterious to many, irresistible to others, can be finicky to prepare, intimidating to purchase, and it can put your wallet on the line. But with a little know-how and confidence, you'll soon be hooked.

Carpe Diem – Fish Of The Day?

Nope, Carpe Diem does not mean "seize the carp" or "catch of the day." It's Latin for "seize the day." And while we're at it, the word "seafood" is not necessarily limited to "fish from the sea." Seafood actually has two meanings according to my online dictionary:

– Edible fish or shellfish from the sea.

– Edible fish (broadly including freshwater fish), shellfish or roe, etc.

The Good Fat

Yes it's true. Not all fat is created equal! I'm not talking about that big old bulge above our belts after a good meal; I'm talking about the fat that we consume. Fish oil has recently garnered increased attention for its health properties. This, of course, is something our grandmothers have always known, but thankfully today's gel tabs are much easier to swallow than a spoonful of cod liver oil! Fish oils are polyunsaturated and are called omega-3 fatty acids. Omega-3 and omega-6 are the two essential fatty acids needed by the body, yet the body can produce neither of them on its own. Omega 6 is readily available in cooking oils, which people in western cultures get in abundance. Omega-3, on the other hand, is lacking in most western diets.

And Then There Were Three

I know I'm spending a bit of time here, but I want you to be armed with information about why fish is so healthy. Next time your teen turns up his nose, you can tell him that research has shown that eating fish such as tuna, salmon and mackerel will help his brain function so he can study more; improve heart efficiency so he can do more exercise; and boost his immune system so he won't miss school. I'm sure he'll be very appreciative and will thank you endlessly!

There are actually three types of omega-3 essential fatty acids: EPA and DHA, found in fish, some meat products and eggs; and ALA found in assorted nuts, seeds, dark green leafy vegetables, and some vegetable oils. By the way, you're onto something if you like sushi rolls; fresh seaweed is a good source of both EPA and DHA.

A Pound Of Fish

Even though there are reams of articles and evidence pointing to the benefits of eating fish, it is estimated that North Americans prepare on average only 15 pounds per person per year at home. However, we eat almost twice that amount in restaurants. This leads me to believe that people just need more information and then they can buy and prepare seafood with confidence. Buying fish need not be an ordeal. Search out a fishmonger who comes with good recommendations. When buying fish look for the following:

Smell: Fish should smell like you're standing beside the ocean, not like you've been in it for a few days.

Appearance: If you're buying a whole fish, it should look like it was just pulled out of the water. The eyes should still be bright; the skin should be firm – not dry and scaling off. If it's a fillet or steak you're after, they should be evenly colored with no brown, mushy spots.

Storage: Fish is an extremely perishable food. Once it's brought home from the store, refrigerate it immediately and cook within two days. If you've bought it frozen, keep it frozen. To thaw, it's best to put the fish in the fridge the night before you're going to cook it, or in a pinch, hold fish under cold running water. Don't use hot water as the heat will start to cook your lighter fish varieties and it will be unevenly thawed.

Tip – If your fish has been in the freezer a bit too long and you want to revive it, try soaking it in milk as it thaws. This will remove some of the freezer taste and help it smell freshly caught again. Discard milk before cooking.

Them Bones

O.K., everybody sing along: "Your toe bone's connected to your foot bone. Your foot bone's connected to your anklebone. Your anklebone's connected to your . . ." All right already, I'll stop! What is it about fish bones? There aren't a lot of them relatively speaking. Not an anklebone in sight. Fish bones are elusive little things. You can get one stuck in your cheek really easily, as they are hard to see. To detect fish bones, run your hand along the uncooked fillet or steak, or even better, drape the fillet over an inverted bowl. That will make the bones protrude upwards. Use a pair of tweezers or needle nose pliers to remove.

Tip – For you forward-thinkers: save the bones from your white fish and make a stock. A fish stock is a wonderful addition to all kinds of soups and sauces. Avoid using fish bones from darker fish like salmon; the stock won't be clear and the broth will be fattier as a result as they are fattier fish to start with.

Just A Tiny Bit Of Science (I promise)

Remember in the pork section we discussed myoglobin, the molecule that transports oxygen throughout the body? The more the animal uses its muscles, the more oxygen is needed to fuel them and the more myoblobin is needed, therefore making the muscle appear red or darker in color. Fish lead a charmed life – no gravity to fight; no legs for walking – so they produce very little myoglobin, making the muscles light in color and translucent in nature.

We've also talked about coagulation in cooked meat, and the same applies to fish. As the fish cooks, water is removed from the molecules and they shrink closer together. This will turn the once-translucent fibers into opaque molecules. See, I kept my promise, that wasn't so bad.

Can't Stand The Heat

Fish has almost no connective tissue, and because of that it is a very delicate meat to cook. A reliable guide for cooking is 10 minutes per inch at its thickest part. Some people like to test its doneness by "flaking" the fish. That will indeed work, however I caution you: by the time it flakes, it's also a bit dry. Instead, you might want to check its coagulation. If the meat looks opaque, then it's generally ready. I like to undercook it slightly, then tent it or let it rest for about 5 minutes. The residual heat in the fish will take care of the rest and tenting will bring the moisture back to the whole fish rather than just its center.

Will You Marinate Me?

Fish takes to a marinade like it takes to water. Start with an acidic property like lemon, add some oil to even it out, throw in some fresh or dried herbs, a bit of salt and pepper and you've got a feast in the making. Sounds almost too good to be true? There's a catch (no pun intended). Because seafood tends to be delicate and lacking in dense connective tissue, it absorbs acids much faster then other meats. So a marinade that contains lemon or vinegar will go to work breaking down fibers at an alarming rate, leaving your fish on the mushy side. And I can speak with absolute authority when I say, *you don't want mushy fish!*

Thirty minutes is all you need to marinate your delicate catch of the day and up to 60 minutes for a denser fish like a salmon or swordfish steak. And please, don't stick to the usual seasonings like dill and onion. Branch out a bit. Try a jalapeño, or chopped tomatoes. Be brave, it won't hurt you, I promise. Unless, of course, you add too much jalapeño. Then you'll have very clear sinuses.

Avoiding Sticky Situations

I'm a huge fan of fish, particularly when cooked on the barbecue. It's not as tricky as it would seem. The key to grilling fish, especially a fragile white fish, is to oil up the grill and make sure it's hot. There's nothing worse than having your fish stick to the grill and then having to scrape it off to eat it. If that happens, try putting a chutney or salsa on top to hide it. As long as it's not grossly overcooked, it should still be salvageable.

I like to cook my fish directly over the flame, but I'll sometimes use a fish basket. It makes turning it over a snap. Again, I caution you: if the fish basket isn't well oiled, the fish will stick to it as well. Some people like to cook fish on a wet cedar plank, which is also great or there are some folks who prefer to make a foil "boat" and cook the fish in this. This method will guarantee that it doesn't stick, but you won't get a nice crust on the fish and you'll lose some of the barbecue taste.

So many fish in the sea, so little time. The varieties and choices of fish are endless. I have to say I have a few favorites. Snapper is one of my favorites; it's light and delicate, yet very versatile. I like snapper done whole, with a jerk marinade, either straight on the grill or with a grill basket. Before cooking, give the fish a few slashes along the thicker part of the back to help the heat penetrate evenly.

Tuna – it's not just for cans! It's perfect for the grill because it's extremely dense. I prefer tuna cooked medium rare. Be careful grilling tuna though; it's extremely lean, so it can dry out very quickly.

I love shrimp, lobster, scallops and crayfish (also known as crawfish or crawdad). Crayfish are great because they're bigger than shrimp, and have the consistency of lobster (they're relatives). You can cook shellfish in its shell, which sort of acts like a little steamer oven; and for us tactile types, it's fun to get in there with your fingers and remove the shells after it's cooked.

Before you dive into the recipes in this section, I want to give you a few tips about cooking shrimp and lobster: They are both incredibly easy to cook, however, the secret is: DO NOT overcook. For perfect shrimp, cook them about 1 1/2 –2 minutes, turning half way through. You'll notice that they will turn pink when done. When using a marinade make sure it isn't left on for more than 30 minutes or the acidic properties (citrus, vinegar, wine, etc.) will cook them and they'll get tough and rubbery.

Shrimp are sold according to how many typically fit in a pound: 8–10 per pound, 16–20 per pound and 21–25 per pound. Your fishmonger will guide you through this process.

I could eat lobster every day. My favorite is the 1 1/2–2 pounder. They tend to be sweet and tender at that size. Leave the lobster in the shell over the barbecue. It will help protect it from the fire and the meat is easy to eat right out of the shell. Some people think that lobster meat is done when it's a bright pink, but I beg to differ. By then it's like shoe leather. Look for a delicate light-pink color. Dip into a butter-based or mayonnaise sauce and you've got yourself a piece of paradise.

Listen my children and you shall hear
Of the midnight ride of Paul Revere,
On the eighteenth of April, in Seventy-five;
Hardly a man is now alive
Who remembers that famous day and year.

He said to his friend, "If the British march
By land or sea from the town to-night,
Hang a lantern aloft in the belfry arch
Of the North Church tower as a signal light, –
One if by land, and two if by sea;
And I on the opposite shore will be, . . ."
– FROM "THE LANDLORD'S TALE; PAUL REVERE'S RIDE"
   BY HENRY WADSWORTH LONGFELLOW

BLACKENED SCALLOPS WITH GUACAMOLE ON TORTILLA CHIPS

Nothing worse than an overcooked scallop. Don't leave these wonderful little taste nuggets on the grill for more than 90 seconds a side. You want them just warmed through in the middle and nice and crusty with the blackened spices on the outside.

12 large sea scallops

1 tbsp Blackening Spice (15mL) (recipe below)

12 large tortilla chips

Guacamole

2 large ripe avocados

Juice of 1 lime

1 medium red onion, finely chopped (30mL)

1 tsp jalapeno pepper, finely chopped (5mL)

1/2 tsp ground cumin (2.5mL)

Salt and pepper to taste (5mL)

1/2 red bell pepper, chopped

1 tbsp chopped cilantro (15mL)

Blackening Spice

1/2 cup paprika (125mL)

1/4 cup salt (60mL)

1/4 cup onion powder (60mL)

1/4 cup garlic powder (60mL)

1/4 cup plus 1 tsp cayenne (65mL)

1/4 cup white pepper (60mL)

2 tbsp black pepper (30mL)

1 1/2 tbsp dried thyme leaves (22mL)

1 1/2 tbsp oregano leaves (22mL)

Directions:

- In a medium bowl, mash avocado flesh with a fork. Add lime juice, onion, jalapeno, cumin, and salt. Mix to combine. Gently fold in bell pepper and cilantro.

- Rinse and dry scallops using a paper towel. Sprinkle liberally with blackening spice on both sides.

- Preheat barbecue to 400F (204C). Oil grill.

- Place scallops directly on grill and cook for approximately 1 1/2 minutes per side. Remove scallops. To serve, place a dollop of guacamole on each tortilla chip and top with a scallop.

Blackening Spice

- In a medium bowl mix all spices together well.

- Store in an air tight jar.

Serves 12 appetizer portions

CEDAR-PLANKED SALMON

Cedar-planked salmon has become something of a Canadian culinary staple. Every high-end restaurant in the country was doing this dish for a while. Make sure you soak the planks for a good long time so they hold on the grill and infuse the salmon with not only a nice cedar flavor, but also a nice super pink color.

3 cedar planks broken into 8 x 6-inch pieces

1 side of Atlantic salmon cut into 8 portions, approx. 6 oz each

Marinade

1/4 cup vodka (60mL)

1/4 cup fresh lemon juice (60mL)

1 tbsp prepared horseradish (15mL)

1 clove garlic, chopped fine

2 tbsp juniper berries (30mL)

2 sprigs fresh thyme

Directions:

- Soak cedar in cold water for 1 hour.

- Mix marinade ingredients and place in sealable plastic bag, add salmon and marinate in refrigerate for 1 hour.

- Preheat barbecue to 400°F.

- Place soaked cedar planks on grill rack until they start to smoke.

- Reduce heat to 300°F and place salmon pieces on to cedar. Close lid on barbecue and cook for approximately 15 minutes. Salmon should have a golden color and flake with ease with clear juices running through. Serve with tarragon mayonnaise (page 226) and enjoy!

Serves 8

CORN HUSK GRILLED RED SNAPPER

I love to do a snapper whole on the barbecue and have tried it many different ways. The way this mild fish absorbs the garlic in this unique recipe adds a new dimension to a staple fish dish.

2–5 lb red snapper, gutted but scales, head and tail left on (1–2.5kg)

1 scotch bonnet pepper, seeds and veins removed

4 cloves of garlic

2 teaspoons of salt, or to taste (10mL)

1/3 to 1/2 cup of red wine vinegar (75 to 125mL)

1/2 cup of chopped fresh parsley (125mL)

3 tablespoons of vegetable oil (45mL)

4 corn husks, silk removed

Directions:

- Combine pepper, garlic, salt, red wine vinegar and cilantro in blender and blend until the mixture is smooth.

- Place red snapper in a nonreactive container and pour paste over fish, coating it well on both sides. Cover and refrigerate for 2 hours.

- While fish is marinating, prepare corn husks. Remove corn from husk, leaving enough of the cob to hold the husk in place. Soak husks in cold water.

- Preheat grill to a medium heat.

- Once fish has marinated, wrap fish with damp corn husks and place on barbecue rack. Cook fish with barbecue lid closed for approximately 10 minutes.

- When the fish is cooked, juices will be bubbling and you will be able to lift out the central bone easily. Serve and enjoy!

Serves 4

CRAB LEGS WITH LEMON-LIME BUTTER

There's not a whole lot you need to do to king crab legs. O.K. we have white wine, garlic, butter and hot pepper flakes. Now that's heaven!

2 lb (1kg) frozen king crab legs, thawed

Lemon-Lime Butter

1 cup butter, melted (250mL)

3 cloves garlic, chopped

Zest of 4 lemons

Juice of 1 large lime

3 tbsp white wine (45mL)

1/2 tsp hot chili flakes (5mL)

1 stalk lemon grass, peeled and chopped

1 tbsp olive oil (15mL)

Directions:

- Preheat grill to 375F (190C) or medium-high heat.
- Rinse crab legs well and place on grill to cook for 4–6 minutes.
- Remove crab legs from grill and serve with lemon-lime butter for dipping.

Lemon-Lime Butter Directions:

- Combine all ingredients in large saucepan. Let simmer over medium high heat until flavors are infused.

Serves 6

"FUN TIME" SHRIMP QUESADILLAS WITH PINEAPPLE AND RED & YELLOW PEPPERS

When fishmongers refer to shrimp as being "16/20", it means that's roughly how many you get per pound. The honey glaze gets pumped with a little orange juice and is a really nice contrast to the cheese filling.

2 lb tiger prawns (16–20/lb), peeled and
    deveined (1kg)
2 tbsp olive oil (30mL)
Salt and pepper to taste
2 red bell peppers
2 yellow bell peppers
1 tbsp vegetable oil (15mL), plus 1 tbsp(15mL)
10 slices pineapple, 1/4-inch thick (6mm)
8 large flour tortillas (8inch/51cm)
1/4 cup vegetable oil for brushing and
    grilling (60mL)

Honey Glaze

1 tsp lemon zest (5mL)
1/3 cup Dijon mustard (125mL)
2 tbsp honey (30mL)
3 tbsp orange juice (45mL)
1 tbsp Worcestershire sauce (15mL)

Cheese Mix

1 jalapeno pepper, finely diced
3 green onions, finely diced
4 cilantro sprigs, leaves only, chopped
5 cups cheddar cheese, grated (1.25L)
Pepper to taste

Directions:

- Place shrimp in a medium bowl. Toss with olive oil and season with salt and pepper.

- In a separate bowl whisk together Honey Glaze ingredients.

- Slice each bell pepper into 6 pieces and remove seeds. Brush each piece with vegetable oil.

- Peel, core and slice fresh pineapple into 1/4-inch (6mm) thick slices and brush with vegetable oil.

- Preheat barbecue to 425F (210C) or high heat.

- Combine Cheese Mix ingredients in a bowl and place in the refrigerator until needed.

- Oil barbecue grate and place shrimp on the grill, cook for 1 minute per side (or until bright pink in color), basting constantly. Remove from grill and let cool. Remove tails from shrimp, slice in half, lengthwise and set aside.

- Reduce barbecue temperature to 350F (175C) or medium heat.

- Oil barbecue grate and place pineapple and peppers on direct heat. Grill pineapple for 1 minute per side or until nice, golden char marks are achieved. Grill the peppers for 1–2 minutes per side. Baste pineapple and peppers constantly with Honey Glaze while grilling.

- Remove from the grill and slice red peppers into small bite size pieces. Slice pineapple into quarters.

- Lightly brush tortillas with vegetable oil. Divide cheese mixture over 4 tortillas and top with shrimp, pineapple and peppers. Cover with another oiled tortilla.

- Reduce barbecue temperature to 250F (120C) or medium-low heat.

- Oil grill grate and place quesadillas down on grill and cook for 4 minutes or until golden brown. Flip quesadilla over and grill for another 4 minutes.

- Remove from grill and slice into wedges.

Yields 16 pieces

GIN-MARINATED GRILLED SHRIMP

Remember to set a timer when marinating the shrimp. You don't want to leave them much more than 30 minutes or they will go rubbery on you.

20 medium-sized shrimp, peeled and
    deveined
1/2 cup vegetable oil (125mL)
1/2 cup gin (125mL)
1/2 cup cilantro, chopped (125mL)
1/3 cup chopped onion (66mL)
1 tbsp garlic, minced (15mL)

Directions:

- Place the shrimp in a large sealable plastic bag. Mix together the remaining ingredients in a bowl and pour into the bag over the shrimp. Toss to coat well and refrigerate for no more than 30 minutes.

- Preheat the grill to high – 400F (205C)

- Remove the shrimp from the marinade. Season with salt to taste. Place the shrimp on the grill and cook until they are no longer translucent on one side, approximately 1–2 minutes. Turn and continue to cook for another minute or two until slightly golden brown and cooked through.

Serves 4

GRILLED CHIPOTLE LIME SHRIMP

A chipotle pepper is a smoked jalapeno in a spicy tomato sauce. They come in cans and can be found in most grocery stores these days. You can easily go up to six cloves of garlic in this recipe if you'd like.

30 tiger prawn shrimps in shell (21–25/lb),
  cleaned, deveined

1 chipotle pepper, chopped

3 cloves garlic, chopped

1 tbsp sugar (15mL)

Juice of two limes

1 cup pineapple juice (250mL)

Salt to taste

Directions:

- Place shrimp in large sealable plastic bag.

- In a medium-sized bowl, mix together the chipotle, garlic, sugar and salt. Add lime and pineapple juice.

- Pour mixture over shrimp and seal baggie.

- Refrigerate for 30 minutes.

- Preheat the grill to 400F (204C) or high heat.

- Oil the grill. Remove the shrimp from the marinade and season with salt and pepper. Place the shrimp on the grill and cook for 2 1/2 minutes, flipping halfway through or until shrimp is pink.

Serves 6

GRILLED CLAMS WITH LEMON BUTTER SAUCE

If you can't find clams, then mussels work in a pinch. Don't forget that when buying clams, the smaller the better. Bigger ones tend to be chewier.

4 lb of clams (2kg) (you can substitute mussels for this recipe)

1/2 cup of butter (125mL)

1/4 cup of white wine (60mL)

2 cloves garlic, chopped

1/2 tsp of freshly ground black pepper (2.5mL)

Directions:

- Preheat barbecue to a high heat.

- Clean and de-beard clams.

- Melt butter in a medium saucepan and add white wine, garlic and pepper and set aside.

- When barbecue is hot, place clams and/or mussels directly on rack and grill until they open, remove and place into a bowl. Discard any shells that do not open.

- Pour warm broth over clams and cover to keep warm.

- Serve hot and with lots of bread to sop up delicious broth.

Serves 8

GRILLED FRESH SARDINES

Sardine is a generic fish that refers to any number of small oily fish. Fresh sardines are an amazing treat when you can find them (depending on where you live). The difference between a fresh and canned sardine is the same as the difference between fresh and canned tuna. It's not even in the same ballpark.

12 fresh sardines, cleaned, head and
    tails left on

1/4 cup coarse sea salt (62mL)

2 tbsp freshly ground black pepper (30mL)

3 tbsp extra virgin olive oil (45mL)

12 lemon wedges

Directions:

- Rinse the sardines under cold water. Drain and blot dry with a clean towel. Pour the olive oil over the sardines and toss them gently to coat. Sprinkle generously with salt and pepper on both sides.

- Preheat the grill to medium high heat. If you can't hold your hand over the heat for "5 steamboats" the grill is too hot. Lower the heat and let it cool a little.

- Cook the sardines for approximately two minutes per side. Serve hot with lemon wedges.

Serves 6

GRILLED LOBSTER WITH SAFFRON-LIME MAYONNAISE

The mayonnaise with the Dijon and basil are incredible on the buttery textured lobster. One of my favorites! This recipe serves a crowd but can easily be cut in half.

10 live lobsters

Pinch of saffron threads (a little goes a long way)

1 cup real mayonnaise (250mL)

2 tsp Dijon mustard (10mL)

4 tsp lime juice (20mL)

Salt and white pepper to taste

1/3 cup olive oil

Directions:

- Place saffron threads in a bowl and pour boiling water over to cover. After 1 minute, once the threads have turned yellow, drain.

- Combine mayonnaise with saffron threads, Dijon mustard, lime juice and salt and pepper. Cover well and chill until needed.

- Preheat grill to 350F (125C).

- If you have to kill the lobster yourself, freeze the lobster for 2 hours, and then plunge them into a pot of salted boiling water for only 2 minutes. Remove the lobster and plunge them into cold water to refresh. Cut them in half. Remove the stomach sac from behind the eyes.

- Brush olive oil over the cut side of each lobster half. Place cut-side-down on grill, cover and grill for 8 minutes or until they are cooked through.

- Serve grilled lobster with saffron-lime mayonnaise.

Serves 20

GRILLED MARLIN WITH COCONUT CHILI CRUST

Make sure the coconut you use is unsweetened. Thai green curry sauce is available in most grocery stores these days.

6 1-inch-thick marlin steaks

Juice of 1 lime

Salt and pepper to taste

2 tbsp olive oil

Coconut Crust

1 cup unsweetened coconut (250 mL)

1 tsp Thai green curry (5 mL)

2 tsp Red Thai finger chili (10 mL)

1 tsp liquid honey (5 mL)

1 tsp chopped ginger (5 mL)

Directions:

- In a medium bowl, combine all ingredients for the crust and mix until well combined.

- Preheat barbecue to medium-high heat 375°F/185°C.

- Drizzle fish with lime juice and season with salt to taste.

- Place the fish on the grill and cook 2-3 minutes, until nice char marks are achieved. Flip and top with Coconut Crust.

- Close BBQ lid and continue to cook a further 4 minutes, until the crust is golden and fish is cooked to medium.

- Serve with Mango Cucumber Salsa (page 219).

Serves 6

ICED OYSTERS OFF THE GRILL

2 dozen oysters, shucked with bottom
    shells and oyster liquor reserved

1 cup bottled clam juice (250mL)

7 tbsp fresh lemon juice (105mL)

4 tbsp extra-virgin olive oil (60mL)

2 tbsp freshly ground black pepper (30mL)

5 cloves garlic, chopped fine

2 tbsp cilantro (30mL)

12 ice cubes

3 cups apple woodchips (750mL)

Directions:

- Place 1 cup of the apple woodchips into a bowl of cold water to soak.

- In a large glass bowl, combine the clam juice, lemon juice, oil, pepper, garlic, and oyster liquor. Place oysters in a large plastic sealable bag and pour marinade over top. Seal the bag and place in the refrigerator for approximately 30–45 minutes.

- Prepare the smoke package. Squeeze the wet woodchips dry and spread them onto a large sheet of aluminum foil. Place the remaining 2 cups of dry woodchips on top and mix them together. Fold the foil around the chips sealing them inside. Using a fork, poke holes in the package on both sides.

- Remove the grill top on the far left of the barbecue and place the woodchip package directly on top of heat source. Turn the burner to the far left of the barbecue to high. Leave the remaining burners off.

- Place the empty oyster shells on a wire rack. Remove the oysters from the marinade and place each one back into a shell. Add a healthy teaspoon of the marinade to each shell. Reserve the remaining marinade to baste the oysters.

- Place the ice in a drip pan. Place the wire rack with the oysters on top of the ice in the drip pan. Place the pan on the right side of the barbecue away from the heat. Let the smoke infuse the oysters for approximately 40 minutes with the lid down.

- Dampen the finished oysters with a touch of marinade and serve warm with lemon wedges and more pepper.

Serves 4

ORIENTAL GRILLED CATFISH

If you can't get your hands on some catfish then you can substitute any meaty whitefish, like a nice piece of tilapia or snapper. The recipe also works with salmon so go ahead and experiment. Remember to oil the grill really well before adding the fish so it won't stick.

6 catfish fillets, 6-8 ounce each (170 –227g)

2 tbsp vegetable oil (30mL)

Marinade

1 cup of light soy sauce (250mL)

2 tbsp peeled and minced ginger (30mL)

2 tsp dried chili flakes (10mL)

2 tbsp white granulated sugar (30mL)

5 cloves garlic, minced

1 tbsp sesame oil (15mL)

2 tsp cracked Szechwan peppercorns (10mL)

Directions:

* Rinse fish under cold water and pat dry. Place the fish in a sealable plastic bag.

* Combine marinade ingredients in a small non-reactive bowl and whisk together. Reserve 1 cup (250mL) of marinade for basting later. Pour the remainder over fish and seal the bag. Place both the fish and the reserved marinade into the refrigerator for 30 minutes.

* Preheat barbecue grill to 375°F (190C) or medium high heat.

* Oil grill grate.

* Remove fish from marinade and discard excess liquid. Pat the fish dry and season lightly with salt and pepper.

* Place the fish on the preheated oiled grill and cook, lid up, for 5–6 minutes per side. Baste with the reserved marinade after flipping. The fish should flake easily. Remove fish from grill.

Serves 6

SCALLOP AND SALMON SKEWERS

The scallops and salmon take the same amount of time to cook so they work well together on a skewer. You can also substitute vermouth for the white wine and lime juice for the lemon.

1 lb sea scallops (500g)

1 lb salmon, cut into 1 1/4" cubes (500g)

12 bamboo skewers, soaked in water

Vegetable oil for grill

Marinade

3/4 cup dry white wine (175mL)

1/3 cup light vegetable oil (75mL)

2 tbsp shallots, minced (30mL)

2 cloves garlic, pressed

Juice from 1/2 a lemon

1/4 tsp salt (1.25mL)

1 tbsp fresh thyme, chopped (15mL)

Directions:

- Combine all marinade ingredients in a ceramic or glass dish and mix well.

- Rinse scallops and cubed salmon with cold water and blot them dry with paper towel. Submerge seafood into marinade and let stand for no longer than 30 minutes.

- Preheat grill to medium-high heat

- Remove seafood from marinade and pat dry. Drain bamboo skewers and thread the scallops and salmon alternately onto skewers.

- Gently oil your grill and place the brochettes onto preheated grill. Cook evenly for approximately 2 minutes per side or until desired doneness. Serve and enjoy!

Serves 4

SKEWERED SCALLOPS WITH PROSCIUTTO

Two favorite things that grill so well with sweet salty proscuitto are scallops and figs, just not at the same time. This simple recipe works really well with a nice balsamic glaze drizzled on the plate. To make the glaze, get yourself a bottle of cheap balsamic (the ten dollar stuff) and boil it down to a thick syrup on the stove top. That's it, easy to make with tons of flavor.

1 1/2 lb sea scallops (750grams)

20 prosciutto slices, paper thin

Coarse salt and pepper

12 bamboo skewers, soaked in water

Directions:

* Preheat grill to medium-high heat.

* Rinse scallops with cold water and blot them dry with paper towel.

* Season scallops with salt and pepper. Place each scallop on a slice of prosciutto and wrap scallop until covered completely.

* Repeat until all scallops are wrapped.

* Thread wrapped scallops onto drained skewers.

* Place on grill and cook for approximately 5 minutes or until prosciutto is golden brown. Serve warm and enjoy!

Serves 4

SNOW BASS IN PARCHMENT

If you're concerned about the over fishing of Chilean sea bass, then ask your fishmonger for another variety like this snow bass. There are hundreds of different species of bass out there, so what do you say we give those little Chilean guys a break?

4 whole 1 lb snow bass, scaled, bones
*   and fins removed*

2 tbsp extra-virgin oil (30mL)

1 stalk of celery, sliced

4 small garlic cloves, sliced paper-thin

1 leek, white part cleaned and thinly sliced

1/4 jalapeno pepper, seeded, minced

1/2 red and yellow pepper, julienned

2 tbsp white wine (30mL)

2 limes, juiced

1/4 cup cilantro leaves (60mL)

Salt and pepper to taste

4 x 8-inch (10cm square) pieces
*   parchment paper*

Aluminum foil

Directions:

- Prepare barbecue for grilling with indirect heat by preheating one side of the grill to 350F (176C) and leaving the other side of the grill off. Place aluminum foil on grill.

- Heat 2 tbsp (30mL) of olive oil on medium heat in a small sauté pan. Add the garlic, shaking the pan constantly to avoid burning. When garlic begins to turn a golden color, remove from the heat. Pour the garlic and oil into another container and set aside.

- Place an 8-inch (10cm) square piece of parchment paper on a flat surface, with one corner facing you. Season the bass with salt and pepper and place in the lower third of the paper.

- Top the fish with 1/2 teaspoon (2.5mL) of garlic and oil, 1/4 of the leeks, celery, bell peppers and jalapeno. Add 1/2 teaspoon (2.5mL) of wine, 1 teaspoon (5mL) lime juice, and 1 teaspoon (5mL) cilantro.

- Fold the paper over the fish and fold the edges over, forming an envelope. Making sure there are no openings. Repeat with the rest of the ingredients to create 4 packages.

- Place fish on cool side of barbecue and grill with indirect heat at 350F (176C) for 25 minutes. Serve the fish in the packages. A delicious gift!

Serves 4

SMOKED PROSCUITTO-WRAPPED CHEESY SHRIMP

This recipe calls for the biggest shrimp you can find this side of a lobster tail. The combination of goat cheese and cream cheese give the dish a rich, smooth texture balanced with sweet roasted garlic and the salty ham.

12 jumbo shrimp, (6–8/lb) peeled
and deveined

1/2 cup cream cheese (125mL)

1/2 cup goat cheese (125mL)

1 tsp pure honey

2 tbsp chives, chopped (30mL)

2 tbsp roasted garlic (30mL)

Salt and pepper to taste

12 sheets prosciutto, thinly sliced

Directions:

- In a medium bowl, mix cheeses, chives, honey, roasted garlic and salt and pepper. Combine well.

- Butterfly the shrimp using a sharp knife (cut shrimp lengthwise 3/4 of the way through, so shrimp opens up like a book).

- Place 1 tablespoon stuffing inside each shrimp, spread evenly.

- Wrap a slice of prosciutto around each shrimp, ensuring the stuffing is not exposed.

- Drizzle shrimp with oil.

- Preheat barbecue to medium heat.

- Place shrimp on well oiled grill.

- Cook for 2-3 minutes per side or until prosciutto is crispy and shrimp is no longer opaque.

- Remove from heat and serve immediately.

Serves 6

WEST INDIAN RUM SHRIMP

First you get to marinate the shrimp in rum and all sorts of spices. Then you get to smoke them with cherry wood. Your guests are going to die from pleasure, and they don't have know how easy it is to make. Just sit back and enjoy the applause.

4 lb large raw shrimp (2kg)

Marinade

2 cups dark rum (500mL)

1/2 cup melted butter (125mL)

3 tbsp honey (15mL)

2 tbsp pure vanilla extract (30mL)

2 tsp ground allspice (10mL)

2 tsp ground cinnamon (10mL)

5 tbsp very finely chopped ginger (75mL)

10 cloves garlic, finely minced

Finely minced zest from 1 lime

1 tbsp Tabasco sauce (15mL)

1 cup cherry woodchips soaked in cold
*   water for 30 minutes*

2 cups dry cherry woodchips

Directions:

- Preheat barbecue to 220°F (110°C).

- Shell and devein shrimp.

- In a small bowl combine marinade ingredients and mix well. Toss in shrimp and coat evenly. Place in the fridge to marinate for as little as 20 minutes to no more than 1 hour.

- Remove the shrimp from the marinade and place in a bowl. Let them come to room temperature; stand for 10 minutes, covered. Shrimp must be at room temperature when smoking.

- Squeeze the water from the wet chips and place them in the center of a large piece of tin foil. Add the dry chips and mix. Fold the foil into a sealed pouch. With a fork, poke holes in both sides of the pouch from which the smoke will escape. The more holes – the more smoke!

- Keep the burner under the woodchip pouch on medium- to high- heat and turn the other burners off. Once the grill is smoking, quickly place the shrimp directly over the grills that are off. Smoke shrimp with indirect heat for 10–15 minutes or until shrimp are evenly pink and slightly caramelized on the outside. Transfer shrimp to a warm serving platter and enjoy!

Serves 4

WILD SALMON WITH RASPBERRY GLAZE

If you can't find wild salmon, then the farmed version will have to do. It's nowhere near as good but it's better than nothing. Of course, fresh is better than pre-frozen salmon. Not true of the raspberries however. While barbecue season offers up tons of fresh berries, the frozen variety with seeds removed actually are easier to work with in making this glaze. Just throw a couple of fresh ones on the plate for garnish.

8 x 6-oz salmon fillet (6 x 170g)

4 tbsp olive oil (60mL)

Salt and pepper to taste

Raspberry Glaze

3 cups frozen raspberries, defrosted (750mL)

2 tsp chopped fresh ginger (10mL)

1/2 tsp smoked paprika

Juice of 1 lemon

1 tbsp sugar (15mL) or to taste

Salt and pepper to taste

Directions:

- Place frozen, defrosted raspberries in a colander set over a bowl. Allow the juice to drain through by pressing down with a spatula. You should have 1 cup (250mL) of juice in a bowl. Discard fruit.

- In a small saucepan combine lemon juice, paprika, ginger, sugar, salt and pepper. Add the reserved raspberry juice and simmer over medium-high heat for 5 minutes. Strain into a bowl and set aside.

- Preheat barbecue to 375F (190C) or medium-high heat. Oil grill.

- Drizzle fillets with oil and season with salt and pepper.

- Place fillets and cook for 2 minutes or until golden char marks are achieved. Baste the trout continuously with the glaze. Flip the fillets and continue to cook and baste for 3 minutes. Remove fish from grill when desired doneness is achieved. Serve and enjoy!

Serves 8

Chicken or Dare

The greasy doorknob, the constant licking of the fingers. He's hooked on this chicken, isn't he?
– JERRY SEINFELD (ABOUT KRAMER) IN "THE CHICKEN ROASTER"

Chicken with Wild West Sauce

Cinnamon Chicken with Nutty Relish

Garlic Rotisserie Chicken

Grilled Chicken Burritos

Grilled Chicken Skewers

Lemon Ginger Drumsticks with Mango Mustard Seed Glaze

Lemon Pepper Cornish Hens

Muffin Tin BBQ Eggs

Orange Tequila Chicken Breasts

Pecan and Dijon-Crusted Chicken

Quail Stuffed with Couscous

Tea-Smoked Chicken

White Wine and Dijon Mustard Whole Chicken

North Americans are hooked on chicken. According to statistics, in 1960 we consumed an average of 28 pounds of chicken per person per year. In 2005, North Americans ate approximately 85 pounds of chicken per person per year. Interestingly, in 1960 total red meat consumption was 131.6 pounds per person and in 2005 it was 112.8 pounds per person. Fish and shellfish went from 10.3 pounds in 1960 to 15.6 pounds in 2005. Notice anything? Despite the fact that red meats are now available in leaner varieties, North American tastes continue to shift away from them.

Chicken Little, Henny Penny, Goosey Poosey and Cocky Locky

Folks, I have to tell you: when it comes to poultry there is so much more than chicken. Some of my favorites are quail, Cornish game hen, turkey and squab. These birds are all terrific on the grill. You can butterfly most of them by taking the bone out of the center to cook flat, or put them on a rotisserie. Marinades, rubs and brines all are excellent methods for barbecuing poultry.

Fowl Play

The chickens we eat in North America today are largely descended from the Southeast Asian red jungle fowl, first bred in India around 2000 B.C. – now Cornish- (British) and White Rock- (American) bred. Cornish hens, capons, hens, roasters and broil-fryers are all chickens with relatively short life spans; from 7 weeks for capons to 1 1/2 years for tougher stewing hens:

Cornish Game Hen: Weight: 1–2 pounds. Great roasted; whole or stuffed.

Capons: Male chickens, the youngest in this list – usually about 7 weeks old. They are surgically unsexed and weigh 4–7 pounds. Tender meat; great roasted.

Roaster: These are the chickens we're most familiar with, and as per the name, they're excellent for roasting whole. Weight: 5-7 pounds. By the way, legs and thighs are underutilized on the barbecue. Too bad, too, because they tend to be fattier, and therefore quite moist when cooked properly

Broil-fryers: Weight: 2 1/2-4 1/2 pounds Young, tender meat. Delicious, using just about any method.

Stewing/baking hen, cock or rooster: Best for low-and-slow cooking or stewing. These are older chickens and therefore not as tender.

A Squab, A Turkey and A Quail Go Into A Grill

Let's not forget the other fowl. Here are a few wonderful varieties I enjoy:

Squab: Also known as game birds, squabs are young pigeons bred for meat. They are usually processed at about 4 weeks of age. (Aren't you glad you're not a squab?) Young, fresh squab meat will look rosy pink in color and have a flexible neck. It should look plump and juicy – definitely not dry. Squab is ideal for high-heat fast grilling – 5 minutes maximum. I like this bird done medium-rare, as it can get way too dry cooked any longer. By the way, an older squab will have darker skin, a smaller neck and be firmer to the touch. They are still edible but require a slower technique with closer attention to basting than the quick-cook younger bird.

Turkey: Thanksgiving turkey done on the barbecue? You bet! The pilgrims did it. It's easy and a very tasty change from the ordinary. You can smoke a turkey, or sear and then cook it slowly, or you can brine it. I personally like the results I get with brine. It tends to plump up the meat and help to retain moisture for slow cooking. A very simple brine includes water, brown sugar, a cinnamon stick and whole star anise. I like to let the bird soak in the brine for at least 24 hours then cook it slowly with a bit of smoke.

Quail: Native to North America, this small game bird eats mostly nuts and seeds. Some say that it is its diet that makes quail so mild flavored and tasty without much manipulation in the kitchen. As a matter of fact, with just a little olive oil, salt and pepper, quick, high-heat grilling for 2–3 minutes per side; it's incredible! If you'd like to use a marinade, an easy one for quail is red wine with just a touch of vinegar, olive oil and/or a dash of sesame seed oil, salt and pepper. Marinate for 30 minutes and mmm, mmm good!

Doctor, Doctor Give Me The News

Unfortunately, poultry – chicken in particular – can be home to some pretty nasty little bugs. The two most prevalent are *salmonella* and *campylobacter*:

Salmonella: Not just one germ but rather a group of bacteria that can be the cause of diarrheal illness in humans. The salmonella bacterium has been identified for over 100 years and is one of the most common forms of food poisoning. The infection usually will cure itself within 5–7 days; however the afflicted person needs to keep a careful eye on avoiding dehydration.

Campylobacter: A group of spiral-shaped bacteria that can afflict both animals and humans. Symptoms include: cramping, diarrhea, fever and abdominal pain, usually noticeable within 2–5 days after exposure to the organism. The bacterium lives at the body temperature of fowl and is thus adapted to birds, who are carriers. The bacterium is delicate and will not tolerate oxygen or drying. Freezing will reduce the number of bacteria on raw meat.

Scrub, Scrub, Scrub

Doesn't all this talk about bacteria in chicken make you want to rush out and get some? Maybe not, you say? Fear not; there is a way to lessen your exposure to these microscopic critters:

Washing: Many people think you should wash chicken before you cook it. You certainly can if you wish. However, washing chicken can potentially spread the bacterium over everything that it touches in the process. A far more effective way to kill off any bacteria present is to ensure that the internal temperature of cooked chicken reach at least 165 F.

Plastic Or Wood?: Much has been written about the plastic vs. wood cutting-board debate. I personally don't want to add volumes to it, however suffice it to say they are both conductors of bacteria. It's a matter of common sense. After using your board for cutting your poultry pieces (not paltry pieces), scrub it down with hot water and soap – white vinegar works really well, too. Every so often, really give your board a serious scrubbing with household bleach and let it air dry.

Not All Chickens Are Created Equal

Just like beef and pork, chickens are subject to the same form of inspection and grading. Inspection of the internal organs for signs of disease is mandatory. Chickens that pass inspection are given a seal of "wholesomeness." To further help the consumer, chickens are also graded on a voluntary basis. **Grade A** chickens are plump, clean, with no broken bones or bruises and no skin discolorations. **Grades B** and **C** have some sort of visible damage, but are still considered healthy and edible. These chickens are often cut for packaging or used for commercial purposes.

Safe Keeping

Most of us are already familiar with buying chicken. But what do you look for when you're at the grocer? Do you simply pick up the Styrofoam package, give it a poke and a shake and put it in your cart? Here are a few tips that might help you:

When chickens are processed, the blood is drained before packaging, and only a very small amount of blood will remain in the muscle tissue. Watch out for an improperly bled chicken, which will tend to have a cherry-red hue to the skin. Usually these chickens are detected at the plant and not passed through.

A small amount of pink-colored fluid in the bottom of the package is normal. This is water that has been absorbed during the chilling process.

Keeping chicken cold will help reduce the spread of bacteria and increase shelf life. Chicken should feel cold to the touch when purchased and can be stored in the fridge for up to 2 days or frozen, ideally no longer than 1 month.

Defrosting is best done slowly either in the refrigerator, in cold water or in the microwave. I'm not keen on microwave defrosting, as it tends to thaw chicken unevenly and you can get cooked bits that will be dry and chewy.

If thawing in the refrigerator, plan ahead. Boneless cuts will thaw overnight, while whole birds will require 2 days or longer. If you choose not to use the chicken that you've defrosted in your fridge, you can safely put it back in the freezer for future use.

For more spontaneous defrosting, put your chicken in an airtight bag and submerge it in a container of cold water, changing the water every 30 minutes to make sure it stays cold. A whole bird will take 2–3 hours and chicken parts will defrost in about an hour. If using this method, definitely cook the chicken before freezing again.

When defrosting in the microwave, care is needed. First set the microwave's heat intensity to its lowest setting. This will still produce heat, so there is a chance the chicken will begin to cook, especially around the edges. Cook chicken immediately to at least 165F.

Never partially cook chicken for later use. If the heating process has been started, cook immediately.

When using a marinade on raw chicken, do not use any leftover marinade on cooked product. If you must, boil it for at least 5 minutes.

Last But Certainly Not Least

Remember to tent your meat after it's been cooked. Go ahead and take it off the grill at around 155F. (For chicken parts, that should take about 15–20 minutes; for a whole bird, about 1–11/2 hours in a barbecue that is at 400–500F.) Leave the thermometer in the meat, cover and let the temperature rise to 165F. Your reward for this last step will be a juicy, succulent meal.

Tip – Backyard barbecues and family reunion cookouts are breeding grounds for food poisoning. When I was a kid, nobody gave much thought to leaving a half-eaten chicken out all day, then saving it for leftovers. For safety's sake, refrigerate cooked chicken after 4 hours. This is especially true for meat that has been stuffed.

Do not be afraid of simplicity. If you have a cold chicken for supper, why cover it with a tasteless white sauce which makes it look like a pretentious dish on the buffet table at some fancy dress ball?
–FROM SIMPLE FRENCH COOKING FOR ENGLISH HOMES (1923) BY
  X. MARCEL BOULESTIN, CHEF AND FOOD WRITER (1878-1943)

CHICKEN WITH WILD WEST SAUCE

Ask your butcher to halve the birds for you. Free range is better than penned, grain fed is better than not. Also, ask for a capon from the butcher instead of a regular chicken for an extra taste treat. Capons are roosters and are bigger than your regular chicken, so they serve more people. If you can, get your hands on smoked paprika for an extra taste dimension.

2 x 3 lb whole chickens, halved

Wild West Paste:

4 tbsp of room temperature butter (60mL)

4 tbsp of Worcestershire sauce (60mL)

2 tbsp of paprika (30mL)

2 tbsp of finely diced canned chipotle
   chili peppers in adobo sauce

1 tsp of dry mustard (5mL)

1 tsp of garlic salt (5mL)

1 tsp of lemon pepper (5mL)

Wild West Basting Sauce:

6 tbsp of Worcestershire sauce (90mL)

3 tbsp of water (45mL)

1 tsp of dry mustard (5mL)

Directions:

- Combine Wild West Paste ingredients and massage the chicken halves thoroughly. Rub the paste inside and out working it as far as possible under the skin without tearing it. Place the chicken halves into plastic bags and refrigerate.

- Remove chicken from fridge and let stand covered at room temperature for about 30 minutes.

- Bring grill to a medium heat (4–5 seconds with hand test).

- Mix Wild West Basting Sauce ingredients and place in a spray bottle or in a dish with a basting brush and set aside.

- Transfer chicken to grill and cook skin-side-up and covered for 20 minutes. Do not flip the chicken during this period. Continue to cook the chicken for an additional 30–40 minutes, turning every 10 minutes and ending with the chicken skin-side-down for a final crisping.

- Brush the chicken with Wild West Basting Sauce about halfway through the cooking process.

Serves 4

CINNAMON CHICKEN WITH NUTTY RELISH

Remember to always barbecue your meats bone-in for extra flavor.

*6 large skinless chicken breasts, bone-in,
pounded to 3/4-inch thick.*

Dry Rub

1 tbsp ground cinnamon (15mL)

1 tsp nutmeg (2.5mL)

1 tsp mustard seed powder (5mL)

1/2 tsp coriander (2.5mL)

1 tsp ground cardamom (5mL)

2 tsp garlic powder (10mL)

1 tsp of kosher salt (5mL)

1 tsp of freshly ground pepper (5mL)

1 1/2 tsp brown sugar (7.5mL)

Directions:

- Combine the Dry Rub ingredients together in a small bowl. Rinse and pat the chicken breasts dry. Dust equal amounts of the rub mixture on each piece of chicken and rub it into the meat. Be sure to rub the mixture into both sides of the chicken breasts. Place chicken breasts on a tray or platter, cover and refrigerate for a minimum of 2 hours up to overnight.

- Combine Nutty Relish ingredients in a small bowl and set aside.

- Preheat the grill to 325F (190C) or medium heat.

- Remove the chicken from the fridge and allow it to come to room temperature while the grill heats.

Nutty Relish

1/4 cup chopped onion, soaked in hot
    water for 20 minutes and drained (60mL)

1 red bell pepper, diced (30mL)

1 yellow bell pepper, diced (30mL)

3 tsp raspberry vinegar (10mL)

2 tsp honey (5mL)

1 cup of roasted and peeled hazelnuts,
    coarsely chopped (250mL)

1 tbsp minced dried mint (15mL)

- Oil the grill liberally. Place the chicken on the grill, skin-side-down. Keep the lid open and a spray bottle with water close by to douse any jumping flames. Grill chicken breasts on each side until opaque and juicy (approximately 6–8 minutes).

- Remove the chicken from the grill and tent with aluminum foil. Let rest for 5 minutes before serving. Serve with Nutty Relish and enjoy!

Serves 6

GARLIC ROTISSERIE CHICKEN

When chefs have a night off, there's nothing they like better to make at home than a simple roast chicken. This recipe is so simple, yet it yields such wonderful results. Save the bones to make stock the next day.

1 lb (500g) whole chicken

4 cloves garlic, peeled

3 tbsp fresh basil, snipped (45mL)

3/4 tsp salt (3.75mL)

1 tbsp olive oil (15mL)

1 tbsp lemon juice (15mL)

Directions:

- In a bowl combine basil, salt, olive oil and lemon juice and set aside.

- Starting at the neck on one side of the breast, slip your fingers between skin and meat, loosening the skin as you go work towards the tail end. Once your entire hand is under the skin, free the skin around the thigh and leg area up to but not around, the tip of the drumstick. Repeat on the other side of the breast.

- Rub basil mixture under skin directly on to meat. Slip garlic cloves under skin, evenly spaced. Cover and refrigerate for 4 hours.

- Using butcher's twine, truss the chicken so that it holds together. It will also cook the meat evenly.

- Place a drip pan in the center under the grill, turn the front and the rear burners on high and leave the middle burner off and preheat to 325F (180°).

- Place the chicken on to the spit according to the rotisserie manufacturer's directions.

- Cook until the skin of the chicken is generously brown and the flesh is cooked through. Every 20 minutes or so, baste the chicken with juices that accumulate on the drip pan.

- When cooked, the chicken's internal temperature should be 180F (90C). Remove chicken from rotisserie, cover with foil and let stand for 10 minutes before carving. Serve and enjoy!

Serves 5

GRILLED CHICKEN BURRITOS

This is a great dish for one of those lazy Sunday evening barbecue buffets where everyone gets to load up their own plate and sit around yakking and laughing. Pork also works really well with this recipe.

1 lb boneless and skinless chicken breast (500grams)

2/3 tsp garlic, minced (3.5mL)

1/2 tsp cumin (2.5mL)

1/4 tsp chili powder (1.25mL)

1/3 tsp salt (2mL)

1 tbsp lime juice (1mL)

4 large flat flour or corn tortillas

1 cup Salsa (250mL) (see Smoked Salsa recipe on page 225)

1 cup sour cream (250mL)

1 cup shredded Monterey Jack cheese (250mL)

1 cup shredded iceberg lettuce (250mL)

1 cup canned black beans, mashed (250mL)

Directions:

- Preheat grill to medium heat.

- Combine garlic, cumin, chili powder and lime juice. Rub chicken with mixture evenly on all sides. Wrap seasoned chicken in a tight foil package and cook on the grill for 20 minutes.

- Remove chicken from foil and grill over open flame for 2 to 3 minutes on each side. Remove chicken from grill and let stand for 5 to 10 minutes.

- Warm tortillas by placing a piece of foil on barbecue and tortillas on top of the foil. While tortillas are warming, slice grilled chicken into 1/2-inch pieces.

- Place a portion of beans, chicken and cheese in the center of each tortilla. Fold each end over the filling and grill until brown.

- Once burrito is grilled on both sides serve seam-side-down with lettuce and sour cream and top with salsa. Serve and enjoy!

Serves 4

GRILLED CHICKEN SKEWERS

Here's one with an Indian twist that comes from the garam masala and the yogurt.
Play around with the quantities to get the spice level you like.

*6 lb (3kg) boneless, skinless chicken
thighs cut into 1-inch cubes*

Juice from 4 limes

1 tbsp salt (15mL)

1/2 cup plain yogurt (125mL)

1 tbsp freshly grated ginger (15mL)

7 cloves of garlic, chopped fine

3 tsp garam masala (15mL)

1/2 tsp freshly ground pepper (2.5mL)

1/2 tsp cayenne (2.5mL)

Extra virgin olive oil

Bamboo skewers

Directions:

- Combine chicken, lime juice and salt in a large bowl and toss until the chicken is well coated. Place the chicken and the liquid into a large, sealable plastic bag.

- In another bowl, combine yogurt, ginger, garlic, garam masala, pepper and cayenne. Mix well and pour over the chicken in the bag. Toss and coat the chicken with the mixture. Seal the bag and refrigerate for 4 hours to overnight.

- Soak bamboo skewers in water for 30–45 minutes.

- Remove the chicken from the refrigerator 1/2 hour prior to cooking time to come to room temperature

- Preheat the grill to medium-high heat.

- Place two or three pieces of chicken on each bamboo skewer. Oil the grill grate and place the skewers on the grill, with the ends off the heat.

- Cook with the lid up for 7 to 8 minutes per side. Serve and enjoy!

Serves 12 appetizer portions

LEMON GINGER DRUMSTICKS WITH MANGO MUSTARD SEED GLAZE

Who would think that mixing mint with mango and mustard would be good? I did, that's for sure – it's not only just good, it's fantastic. If your recipe calls for you to rinse or brush off your marinated chicken, try putting it in a colander or on a wire rack in the sink. This will help make clean-up easier.

16 chicken drumsticks

Marinade

1/4 cup fresh grated ginger (60mL)

2 tbsp garlic, minced (30mL)

1 tsp chili powder (5mL)

Juice and zest of 2 lemons

1/4 cup chopped fresh mint (60mL)

1 tsp cracked pepper (5mL)

Directions:

- Using a sharp knife cut 1/4-inch deep diagonal slashes on each side of the drumstick (approximately 3 slashes per drumstick).

- Place slashed chicken into a large sealable plastic bag. Combine marinade ingredients in a small bowl. Pour the marinade over chicken. Seal the bag and refrigerate for a minimum 1 hour and up to 4 hours.

- Preheat grill to 350F (175C) or medium heat.

- Oil grill. Remove chicken from marinade and brush off excess liquid. Season chicken with salt and pepper to taste.

- Place chicken on grill and cook for a total of 12 minutes, basting with Mango Mustard Seed Glaze every few minutes. Turn the chicken legs every three minutes.

Mango Mustard Seed Glaze

1/2 cup commercial mango chutney (125mL)

2 tbsp mustard seeds (30mL)

Salt and pepper to taste

Serves 8

Glaze Directions:

- To prepare glaze, strain the mango chutney with a fine sieve into a small saucepan and warm the liquid over low heat with 1 tablespoon (15mL) water. Mix in mustard seeds and season with salt and pepper.

LEMON PEPPER CORNISH HENS

Whatever you do, don't overcook these delicious birds. They dry out really quickly. Follow the recipe times closely and then make sure you tent the birds with tin foil after cooking for about 15 minutes so the meat will relax and the juices flow back into the entire hen.

4 Cornish game hens, 1.5 pounds each (680g)

2 lemons and zest

2 tsp red pepper flakes (10mL)

1 tbsp chopped garlic (15mL)

1 tbsp Worcestershire sauce (15mL)

1 tsp dry mustard powder (5mL)

1/4 cup vegetable oil (60mL)

Salt and pepper to taste

8 x 14-inch (35cm) flat metal skewers

Directions:

- In medium bowl mix together garlic, Worcestershire sauce, dry mustard, red pepper flakes and vegetable oil.

- Zest the lemons and add to the bowl of marinade ingredients. Peel lemon, remove the white pith from lemon and discard. Chop the peeled lemon into small 1/2-inch pieces (8 mm) and add to the bowl.

- Remove backbone from game hens using poultry scissors.

- Flatten hens by pushing a skewer horizontally through the wings and breast. Push another skewer horizontally though the thighs. Repeat with remaining hens. Place the chicken on a large baking tray.

- Pour marinade over hens turning to coat. Cover and refrigerate for 3 hours.

- Preheat barbecue 250F (125C) or medium high heat and oil grill.

- Season the hens with salt and pepper to taste.

- Place hens skin-side-down on grill and cook for 15 minutes or until the skin is crispy and golden-brown in color. Flip the hens using the skewers as an aid. Continue to cook a further 10 minutes or until there is no trace of pink at the bone.

- Remove from barbecue and tent loosely with foil. Let meat rest 10 minutes.

- Remove skewers and carve the hens into desired portions.

Serves 6

MUFFIN TIN BBQ EGGS

Breakfast on the barbecue! Pair this up with some smoked Canadian back bacon, a side of grilled hash browns and some strong coffee and you've got the perfect summertime backyard brunch.

12 eggs

Non-stick cooking spray

1/2 cup shallots, finely chopped (125mL)

1/2 cup red pepper, finely diced (125mL)

1/3 cup finely diced chives (75mL)

Salt and pepper to taste

Directions:

* Preheat the grill to medium-high heat. Spray a 12-cup muffin tin with non-stick spray, being sure to coat each cup.

* Crack a single egg into each muffin cup. Sprinkle the egg with finely diced shallots, red pepper and chives.

* Season lightly with salt and pepper, cover loosely with foil, place the tin on the grill and close the lid. Cook for approximately 2–4 minutes until desired doneness. Serve hot.

Serves 6

ORANGE TEQUILA CHICKEN BREASTS

Orange juice and tequila not only make a great summertime drink, they work really well together in a marinade. Throw in some chili flakes, a bit of vinegar, lime juice and mint and you've got a killer barbecue dish that takes no time to prep or to grill.

10 large chicken breasts, skinless and
 boneless

1/3 cup brown sugar (75mL)

1/3 cup unseasoned rice vinegar (75mL)

1 tsp dried chili peppers (5mL)

Zest and juice of 4 oranges

Directions:

- In a medium bowl, whisk together the sugar, vinegar and chili pepper and add the remaining ingredients.

- Rinse the chicken in cool water and pat dry.

- Place chicken breasts in a large sealable plastic bag. Pour all but 1/4 cup (60mL) of the marinade over the chicken. Seal the bag ensuring the chicken is well coated. Refrigerate for 3–6 hours.

3 tbsp tequila (45mL)

1 1/2 tsp fresh lime juice (7.5mL)

1/2 cup olive oil (125mL)

1 1/2 tsp fresh mint leaves, chopped (15mL)

1/4 tsp salt (1.25mL)

- Preheat one side of the grill to 375F (190C)or medium-high heat. Leave other side of the grill off.

- Oil the grill. Place chicken over the direct heat and sear chicken until golden brown char marks are achieved on one side only (about 2 minutes). Flip the chicken and move over to side of grill without heat, continue to cook for 6–8 minutes, or until juices run clear.

- Remove chicken, cover loosely with aluminum foil. Let rest for 5 minutes before serving.

Serves 10

PECAN AND DIJON-CRUSTED CHICKEN

You can substitute pretty much any hard nut for the pecans if you're so inclined.
This dish also kicks without the Cajun spice.

8 boneless skinless chicken breasts

2 tbsp olive oil (30mL)

Salt and pepper to taste

Directions:

- To make the crust, combine all the ingredients in a food processor. Pulse until well combined and a chunky paste has formed. Set aside until time to grill.

- Prepare barbecue for grilling with indirect heat by preheating one side of the grill to 250F (125C) or medium-low heat and leaving the other side of the grill off.

Crust

1 cup of vegetable oil (250mL)

3 cups crushed corn flakes (750mL)

1 cup toasted pecans (250mL)

1/4 cup Dijon mustard (60mL)

2 tbsp liquid honey (30mL)

2 tbsp Cajun spice (30mL)

2 tbsp fresh chopped thyme (30mL)

- Oil the grill. Drizzle chicken with olive oil and add salt and pepper to taste.

- Place chicken on heated side of grill and sear each side for 1 minute or until nice char marks are achieved.

- Move chicken over to the non-heated side of the barbecue. Coat the top side of the chicken breasts with crust mixture. Close the barbecue lid and cook for 8 minutes per side.

- Remove chicken and serve with spicy mayo and crusty buns.

Serves 8

QUAIL STUFFED WITH COUSCOUS

Ask your butcher to debone the quail for you. It's a lot of work to do yourself, and they're pretty delicate. Remember this is a dark meat bird so you can serve it on the medium side. An overcooked quail is to cry for.

12 quails, deboned

2 cups oak woodchips soaked in water

1 cup dry oak woodchips

24 bamboo skewers soaked in water for 1 hour

Marinade

1/2 cup red wine (125mL)

Zest of two oranges

4 bunches thyme, chopped

2 tsp pepper (10mL)

Couscous

1 cup couscous (250mL)

1 cup orange juice (250mL)

2 green onions, chopped

1/4 cup raisins (60mL)

2 tbsp tasted pine nuts (30mL)

Salt and pepper to taste

Directions:

- In a large bowl whisk together marinade ingredients.

- Place the quail in sealable plastic bags. Using 1/2 cup (125mL) of marinade, pour it over the quails and seal. Reserve leftover marinade. Refrigerate quail for 1 hour.

- Place 2 cups (500mL) of woodchips in water and soak for one hour.

- Prepare couscous (see below). Stuff quail with cooled couscous.

- "Spatchcock" or flatten the quail by pushing one skewer horizontally through the wings and breast. Push another skewer horizontally throughout the thighs. Repeat with the remaining birds.

- Preheat one side of barbecue to 230F (110C) or medium-low heat. Leave the other side of the barbecue off.

- To build a smoke pouch, drain wet woodchips and squeeze excess water out. Spread wet woodchips on a large piece of aluminum foil. Place 1 cup (250mL) of dry woodchips on top and mix together. Close the foil around the chips to make a sealed pouch. Use a fork to puncture holes on both sides of the pouch.

- Place smoke pouch under heated side of the grill, close lid and wait for smoke.

- When smoke is billowing from the barbecue, place quail on cool side of grill and smoke for 45 minutes.

- Remove quail from grill and tent with foil. Let rest for 10 minutes. Serve and enjoy!

Couscous directions:

- Heat orange juice over medium heat until almost bubbling.

- Place couscous in large bowl.

- Pour hot orange juice over couscous and stir. Cover with plastic wrap and let sit 10 minutes. Fluff with fork, add green onions, raisins, pine nuts, salt and pepper.

- Allow to cool.

Serves 6

TEA-SMOKED CHICKEN

Regular peppercorns will work in a pinch if you can't get your hands on the Szechwan variety. Also, substitute rice wine vinegar if you don't have any sake.

4-5 lb whole chicken

4 cups apple woodchips (1000mL)

1/2 cup black tea leaves (120mL)

Directions:

- For the marinade, crush peppercorns in a spice grinder or a mortar and pestle. In a small bowl combine the remaining ingredients. Put chicken in a large, sealable plastic bag. Pour the marinade over the chicken and rub the inside cavity of the chicken with the marinade. Seal the bag and place in the refrigerator. The chicken should marinate for 24 hours.

Marinade

1 1/2 tsp Szechwan peppercorns, (7mL)

2 tbsp brown sugar, packed (30mL)

2 tbsp sake (30mL)

2 green onions

1 tbsp fresh ginger root peeled and
    minced (15mL)

1 stalk lemongrass, chopped fine

2 tsp salt (10mL)

Tea Glaze

1/2 cup brewed strong black tea (125 mL)

3 tbsp soya sauce (45 mL)

3 tbsp liquid honey (45 mL)

2 tbsp rice wine vinegar (30 mL)

1 tbsp sesame oil (15 mL)

- Prepare 2 smoke pouches. Place 2 cups (500mL) of woodchips into a bowl of cold water to soak for 1 hour (if using a charcoal grill, soak all chips and place over charcoal). On 2 sheets of aluminum foil combine drained wet woodchips with remaining dry woodchips. Combine tea leaves equally between packages. Seal up pouch and pierce multiple times with the tines of a fork, resulting in many holes for the smoke to escape.

- Mix ingredients of the Tea Glaze in a medium bowl.

- Preheat one side of the grill to high heat and place one smoke pouch directly over the heat source. Once bbq is smoking, place the chicken on the side of the bbq without direct heat.

- Smoke the chicken over indirect heat for 2-2 1/2 hours or until meat thermometer reaches 170°F, replacing the smoke pouch halfway through. Baste the chicken three times over the course of its cooking time.

- Remove chicken from the grill and let rest. Serve with Plum Chutney (see page 223).

Serves 4-6

WHITE WINE AND DIJON MUSTARD WHOLE CHICKEN

When making this recipe, remember: for every measure of white wine you put in the marinade – double it for your tummy.

1 whole chicken, 3–4 lbs (1.5–2 kg)
flattened (back bone removed)

Marinade

2/3 cup dry white wine (150mL)

1/3 cup extra virgin olive oil (75mL)

Juice from 1 lemon

4 cloves garlic, pressed

3 tbsp Dijon mustard (45mL)

1 tsp fresh ground black pepper (5mL)

2 tbsp rosemary, chopped (30mL)

Olive oil for rub

Directions:

- Combine the marinade ingredients in a non reactive container and mix well. Place flattened chicken in the marinade, cover and refrigerate for 4 hours.

- Remove chicken from container and discard marinade. Pat chicken dry and rub with olive oil to coat.

- Preheat grill to 350F (175C).

- Once the grill is hot, turn off middle burner and lower the other(s) to medium. Place the chicken, breast-side down over the burner that is off. Close lid and grill for 20 minutes. Turn the chicken over to balance cooking. Cook for another 25 minutes or until the juices run clear.

- Remove from grill, cover with foil and let stand for 10 minutes before carving. This will let the flesh reabsorb its juices. Serve and enjoy!

Serves 4

Dessert Anyone?

Life is uncertain. Eat dessert first.
–AMERICAN AUTHOR ERNESTINE ULMER

Chocolate Fondue with Grilled Peaches and Pears

Cinnamon Toast Fruit Kabobs

Grilled Nectarines with Ice Cream

Grilled Pineapple

Dessert on the grill? Caramelized beef with a cream-based barbecue sauce? No, absolutely not! Grilled fruit and simple sauces make for the perfect ending to a barbecue dinner. Plus, they are an excellent treat . . . even better than grilled veggies – honestly!

"Why should I bother grilling dessert, if I can go down to my local bakery and get a nice pastry, or just dole out scoops of ice cream from the freezer?" Sure, that's simple enough, but there are so many choices of fruits to cook on the grill for a great dessert, and I think you'll be surprised to learn how easy they are to prepare. Remember, your barbecue is nothing if not an alternative heat source to your oven. Don't be intimidated.

Mush, Mush

Avoid mush at all cost. I'm not talking about a team of dog sledders here, or a really sappy movie. I'm talking about pineapple left on the grill for so long that it has to be scraped off. For grilling fruit – pineapple, nectarines, pears and the like – you want to just lightly touch it to the barbecue. Get a few grill marks, heat it slightly and then – perfection!

Top your grilled fruit with a scoop of ice cream or a drizzle of caramel sauce, and maybe some roasted pecans. Yes, I say! For another delicious topping, combine a bit of dark rum (Jamaican is my favorite), with some butter over high heat, boil it down slightly and pour over the fruit. There is nothing better!

Keep It Clean

Most importantly, make sure you clean the grill and oil it thoroughly before you put your fruit on it. You don't want your delicately grilled peaches to taste like buffalo meat. Or maybe you do.

"Stressed" spelled backward is "desserts." Coincidence? I think not!
–AUTHOR UNKNOWN

CHOCOLATE FONDUE WITH GRILLED PEACHES AND PEARS

Now we're talking my language. I love chocolate. I'll wrestle anyone for a chocolate bar or two. This recipe will not disappoint you, my fellow chocoholics – and you know who you are! This is for you. When grilling fruit with skin on it, grill skin-side-up first, then flip. This will help the fruit remain intact.

10 oz of your favorite fondue chocolate, coarsely chopped (1 1/4 cups)

2 ripe pears, sliced into thick wedges

2 ripe peaches, halved and pitted

Other fruit (bananas, apples, strawberries, pineapple and plums) can be substituted

Directions:

- Prepare and preheat grill to low heat.

- In a metal bowl set over a saucepan of barely simmering water (bain-marie) melt the chocolate, stirring to ensure that the chocolate does not over cook.

- Once chocolate is melted, remove the bowl from the pan, and transfer to fondue pot. Place over candle or fondue burner.

- Place cut fruit on grill for approximately 1 minute per side. Remove fruit from grill and serve with fondue forks to dip into chocolate. Enjoy!

Serves 2

CINNAMON TOAST FRUIT KABOBS

These kabobs make a great dessert, but why not use the barbecue for breakfast?

1/4 cup sugar (60mL)

1 tsp ground cinnamon (5mL)

1/4 cup butter, melted

8 x 2-inch thick slices of fresh whole
*   wheat bread*

1 pint (2 cups) strawberries, cleaned
*   and cut into halves*

2 firm bananas, peeled and sliced into
*   even rounds*

1 tbsp vegetable oil to grease the grill (15mL)

Bamboo or metal skewers

Directions:

- Preheat the grill to 300F (150C).

- In a medium-sized bowl, combine the sugar and cinnamon.

- If using bamboo skewers soak them in water for 10–15 minutes.

- Cut the bread into 2-inch cubes and brush them lightly with melted butter. Then gently toss the bread cubes in the cinnamon sugar to coat evenly.

- Thread the cubes on to the skewers alternating with the strawberries and bananas.

- Lightly oil the grill with vegetable oil. Grill the kabobs for 8–10 minutes, turning occasionally until the bread is lightly toasted and browned.

Serves 4

GRILLED NECTARINES WITH ICE CREAM

Nectarines are one of my favorite fruits and they hold up really well on the grill. Leave the skins on to keep them from falling apart. Substitute peaches for the nectarines, if you like, and whipped cream works just as well as ice cream here.

10 nectarines, halved and pitted

2 tbsp honey (30mL)

juice of 1 lime and 1 lemon

1 pt French vanilla ice cream (500mL)

Directions:

- Preheat the barbecue to 350F (176C) or medium.
- In a small bowl mix together the honey and juice.
- Brush the cut sides of the nectarines with honey-juice mixture.
- Oil grill.
- Place the nectarines cut-side-down on the grill. Cook until the fruit is warm and lightly charred. This should only take 2–3 minutes.
- Remove nectarines from the grill and place on a serving tray.
- Serve hot with a scoop of vanilla ice cream.

Serves 6

GRILLED PINEAPPLE

Maple syrup is not just for pancakes. It is a great substitute for sugar and caramelizes beautifully on the grill. Careful not to leave this one on too high or for too long! You don't want charred mush!

2 pineapples, peeled and quartered
  lengthwise
1 cup maple syrup (250mL)
1 tsp of cinnamon (5mL)
1/2 tsp of ground cloves (2.5mL)

Directions:

- Peel and quarter pineapple and place in a plastic bag. Add maple syrup, cinnamon and cloves. Marinate for 2 hours or up to 24 hours.

- Heat grill to medium-high.

- Place pineapple on grill and cook until nicely brown on all sides, turning every 3 minutes and watching carefully not to burn.

- Serve hot with vanilla ice cream and any remaining marinade drizzled over top.

Serves 8

Odds and Sauces

A well-made sauce will make even an elephant or a grandfather palatable.
– ALEXANDRE BALTHASAR LAURENT GRIMOD DE LA REYNIÈRE,
   THE WORLD'S FIRST RESTAURANT CRITIC

Cilantro Radish Relish

Cucumber Dip

Hot Mint BBQ Sauce

Hot Tomato-Based BBQ Sauce

Mango Cucumber Salsa

Martini Relish

Mustard BBQ Sauce

Peach Chutney

Plum Chutney

Smoked Guacamole

Smoked Salsa

Spicy Vinegar-Based BBQ Sauce

Tarragon Mayonnaise

Tomato BBQ Sauce

A homemade sauce or marinade can turn an ordinary piece of meat into a masterpiece on the grill. And the same cut of meat can taste entirely different – savoury, citrusy, spicy, sweet or a combination of some or all of these flavors – depending on the marinade used in preparing it.

Salsas, chutneys and relishes add a little extra flavor to those succulent dishes you've cooked on the grill. "Fresh" is the key word here – always buy fresh ingredients when you can. For many of us, barbecue season coincides with the summer harvest, so finding fresh cucumbers, tomatoes, herbs and fruits shouldn't be a problem. If you're lucky, you might even have your own garden with all the makings for a delicious salsa. For large quantities, or if barbecuing in the "off-season," certain canned ingredients are perfectly acceptable – like canned tomatoes for instance. In the height of the season, though, tomatoes fresh off the vine are a slice of heaven.

Why not skip the condiment aisle at the grocery store and try some of these recipes for barbecue sauces, relishes and salsas instead? There is nothing like a sweet Plum Chutney on Tea-Smoked Chicken or a Cilantro Radish Relish on fish off the grill. Mmmm . . . I'm starting to get hungry.

Never trust a skinny cook
–UNKNOWN

CILANTRO RADISH RELISH

1 bunch fresh cilantro

1 bunch of radishes

1 large white onion

2 tbsp honey

2 tbsp white cider vinegar

Directions:

- Rinse cilantro under cold running water, blot dry with paper towels and pluck the leaves from the stem. Coarsely chop leaves.

- Rinse and trim radishes and cut them into 1/4-inch cubes. Cut onion into 1/4-inch cubes.

- Combine the honey and vinegar in a serving bowl. Add cilantro, radish and onion, and toss to mix. Relish is best served within 2 hours of preparing.

Serves 8

CUCUMBER DIP

Refreshing cucumber mixed with fresh garlic and yogurt. Put that over just about anything – I even love it as a chip-dip substitute. The mint in this recipe gives it a decidedly Middle Eastern flare.

2 cucumbers, peeled and seeded

2 tsp sea salt (30mL)

6 tbsp fresh mint leaves, finely chopped (90mL)

3 cloves garlic, minced

1 tsp sugar (5mL)

1 1/2 cups plain yogurt (regular or low fat) (375mL)

3 tbsp chives, finely chopped (45mL)

Directions:

- Peel the cucumber completely and cut into quarters. Use a spoon to scoop out the seeds. Dice the cucumber into 1-inch cubes. Place the cucumbers in a strainer and sprinkle them generously with sea salt. Place a bowl underneath the strainer to catch the liquid. Leave to drain for 15–25 minutes.

- Meanwhile, combine the mint, garlic, sugar and yogurt in a medium-sized bowl. Set aside in the refrigerator until ready to use.

- Drain the cucumber and rinse well. Pat the cucumber dry with paper towel and add to the yogurt mixture. Add the chives and mix gently. Leave in the fridge to let the flavors combine until ready to serve. This will keep in the fridge for up to 2 days. Serve cold.

Yields 1 cup

HOT MINT BBQ SAUCE

1 cup store bought barbecue sauce
(250mL)

1/2 cup mint jelly (125mL)

1 tbsp hot sauce (15mL)

1 tbsp lemon juice (15mL)

1 tbsp lime juice (15mL)

1/4 cup fresh cilantro, chopped (60mL)

Salt to taste

Directions:

- In a medium saucepan combine all ingredients except the cilantro and salt. Bring to a gentle boil over low heat.

- Allow sauce to simmer for 5 minutes. Remove from heat and stir in the cilantro and salt to taste.

Yields 2 cups

HOT TOMATO-BASED BBQ SAUCE

3 tbsp vegetable oil (45mL)

1 medium onion, minced

4 cloves garlic, minced

1/2 cup ketchup (125mL)

1/2 cup tomato sauce (125mL)

1 cup water (250mL)

3 tbsp cider vinegar (45mL)

3 tbsp Worcestershire sauce (45mL)

2 tbsp of fresh lemon juice (30mL)

1 tsp of your favorite hot sauce (5mL)

1/2 tsp of liquid smoke (2.5mL)

3 tbsp of firmly packed dark brown sugar (45mL)

3 teaspoons of dry mustard (15mL)

1/2 tsp of freshly ground black pepper (2.5mL)

1/3 cup of apple sauce (75mL)

Salt to taste

Directions:

- Heat oil in a large saucepan over medium heat, add onions, and garlic and sauté over low heat until soft and translucent.

- Stir in ketchup, tomato sauce, water, cider vinegar, Worcestershire sauce, lemon juice, hot sauce, liquid smoke, sugar, dry mustard, apple sauce and black pepper and bring to a boil. Reduce heat to low and simmer uncovered for approximately 15 minutes or until the sauce has thickened.

- If the sauce becomes too thick add a tablespoon of water.

- Remove from heat and season with salt and pepper, sugar and a splash of vinegar to taste. This sauce will keep for several weeks when covered tightly and stored in the refrigerator.

Yields 3 cups

MANGO CUCUMBER SALSA

I love to cook with mangos. They are such a versatile fruit. Even when they're not ripe, they're great!

2 cups mango, peeled and chopped (500 mL)

2 cups cucumber, peeled and chopped (500 mL)

1 1/4 cup chopped red bell pepper (315 mL)

1/2 cup red onion, diced (125 mL)

1/3 cup chopped fresh cilantro (83 mL)

3 tbsp lime juice (45mL)

1 jalapeno pepper, seeded and minced

Salt

Freshly ground black pepper

Directions:

- In a large bowl mix the mango, cucumber, red pepper, shallots, cilantro, lime juice and jalapeno.

- Season to taste with salt and pepper. Serve and enjoy.

Yields 5 cups (1250mL)

MARTINI RELISH

1/2 cup kalamata olives, chopped and
    pitted (125 mL)

1/2 cup nicoise olives, chopped and pitted
    (125 mL)

1/2 cup Sicilian stuffed olives, chopped
    and pitted (125 mL)

1/2 red onion, chopped fine (125mL)

1 tbsp olive oil (15mL)

1 tbsp red wine vinegar (15mL)

5 leaves fresh basil, chopped

1 tsp fresh thyme, chopped (5mL)

2 tbsp vermouth (30mL)

Fresh pepper to taste

Directions:

• Combine all ingredients in a medium-sized bowl.
  Stir well. Cover and refrigerate for 2–3 hours.

• Serve with crusty bread.

Yields 2 cups

MUSTARD BBQ SAUCE

1/2 cup Dijon mustard (125mL)

1/2 chipotle pepper, chopped

3 tbsp honey (45mL)

1 tbsp cider vinegar (15mL)

1 tbsp grainy mustard (15mL)

Pinch of tumeric

Pepper to taste

2 cloves garlic, roasted

Directions:

- In medium sized bowl whisk together all ingredients but garlic.

- Squeeze 2 cloves of roasted garlic on to a board and mash into a paste with the side of a knife. Add to sauce and mix.

- Cover with plastic wrap

- Let mixture rest for at least 2 hours before serving.

Yields 1 1/2 cups

PEACH CHUTNEY

Peaches have such a short growing season. Such a shame! Grilled, fresh, pureed, frozen, canned, over ice cream, under ice cream – they are sheer perfection!

8 peaches, pit removed and halved

Juice of 1 lemon

1 tsp ginger, minced (15mL)

1 onion, sliced

1/4 tsp allspice (1mL)

1/4 tsp cinnamon (1mL)

1 tbsp cider vinegar (15mL)

1/4 cup white wine (60mL)

1 tbsp olive oil (15mL)

Marinade

1/2 cup bourbon (125mL)

1 tbsp honey (15mL)

1/2 cup pure maple syrup (125mL)

1/4 tsp fresh nutmeg (1mL)

1 tsp fresh black pepper (5mL)

2 tbsp sugar (30mL)

Cedar planks soaked in water for 1 hour

Directions:

- Combine marinade ingredients in a saucepan and simmer for 10 minutes or until mixture thickens

- Squeeze lemon juice over peach halves and brush peaches with marinade. Cover peaches in plastic wrap and refrigerate for 3 hours.

- Preheat grill to 375F (190C).

- Place cedar planks on grill, close lid and wait until the edges of the planks start to char and smoke.

- Reduce heat to 325F (162C). Place peaches cut-side-down on planks. Grill for 5 minutes. Remove and let cool.

- Chop grilled peaches and place in bowl.

- Preheat skillet to medium. Add onion and ginger. Sauté until onion is slightly softened. Add cinnamon, cider vinegar and white wine.

- Remove from heat and add to chopped peaches. Serve with pulled pork.

Serves 8

PLUM CHUTNEY

1/2 lb each of yellow and red plums,
   ripe but still firm

1 large gala apple

2/3 cup honey (225mL)

6 tbsp white wine vinegar (90mL)

1 tbsp minced peeled fresh ginger (15mL)

1 tbsp chopped garlic (5mL)

2 tsp grated orange zest (30mL)

2 tsp nutmeg (10mL)

2 whole cinnamon sticks (10mL)

Directions:

- Halve and pit the plums. Dice into 1/2-inch cubes. You should have 3 cups (750mL) of diced plums. Place into a bowl.

- Halve apple. Dice into 1/2-inch cubes. You should have 1 cup of diced apple.

- Place water and honey in a saucepan. Stir to dissolve and then bring to a boil. Add vinegar, ginger, garlic and half of the diced plums and the diced apple.

- Bring mixture to a boil and cook for 5 minutes.

- Add the remaining plums, orange zest and spices. Bring to a gentle boil and cook for 10 minutes or until thick and syrupy.

- Remove from heat and let cool. Discard cinnamon sticks. Serve with Tea Smoked Chicken (page 201).

Yields 2 Cups (500mL)

SMOKED GUACAMOLE

2 large red bell peppers

4 smoked Serrano chilies

1/2 small red onion finely chopped

1/2 cup finely chopped fresh cilantro
(125mL)

1 tsp of salt (5mL)

1/2 tsp black pepper (2.5mL)

Juice of 1 lime

3 large, ripe avocados

2 cups dry hickory woodchips

1 cup hickory woodchips, soaked for
30 minutes

Directions:

- Remove grill from barbecue and preheat to a medium heat.

- Prepare a smoke package. Squeeze the excess water from the soaking woodchips and place in the center of a large piece of tin foil. Add the dry chips to the wet and mix them together. Fold the foil around the chips to create a well-sealed package. Using a fork, poke holes on both sides of the smoke package. Set aside.

- Half and remove the seeds from the peppers and chilies. This will remove some of the heat from the hot peppers.

- Place the woodchip package directly on top of the flame where the grill grid has been removed. Turn the other burners off. Place the pepper and chili halves on the grid over the burners that are off.

- Close barbecue lid. Smoke the peppers and chilies for approximately 10 minutes, or until the flesh is charred.

- The skin can now be removed easily. Once skin has been removed and discarded. chop peppers and chilies well and add to a bowl. Add onion, cilantro, salt, pepper, lime juice. Combine mixture well.

- Pit and peel avocados. Add to mixture and mash until incorporated but still chunky. Cover and chill until ready to use, but return to room temperature when ready to serve.

Yields 4–6 serving portions

SMOKED SALSA

You can make a salsa out of just about any fruit or veggie. This combination reminds me of a night on the ranch, with a smokey fire and the sting of the peppers.

6 large tomatoes

4 smoked Serrano chilies

1/2 cup water (125mL)

2 tbsp balsamic vinegar (30mL)

Salt to taste

3 tbsp dried cilantro (45mL)

Mesquite and hickory woodchips soaked
*   in cold water for 30 minutes*

Directions:

- Remove grill from barbecue and preheat to a medium heat.

- Half and remove the seeds from the tomatoes and hot peppers. This will remove the bitter taste from the tomatoes and some of the heat from the hot peppers.

- Drain mesquite and hickory woodchips and set aside.

- Place tomato and hot pepper halves on to the grill. Once the barbecue reaches a medium heat place grill on barbecue along with damp woodchips and close barbecue lid.

- Process will only take approximately 10 minutes, or until the flesh of the tomatoes and peppers are charred.

- Once charred, the skins of the tomatoes and peppers can be easily removed.

- Dice up tomatoes and peppers; add to blender with water, balsamic vinegar and salt. Pulse to a desired chunkiness, add dried cilantro (or fresh, if available) and voila! Serve and enjoy!

Yields 4–6 serving portions

SPICY VINEGAR-BASED BBQ SAUCE

2 cups cider vinegar (500mL)

1 1/4 cups water (310mL)

1/3 cup brown sugar (83mL)

6 tsp salt, or to taste (30mL)

5 tsp hot red pepper flakes (25mL)

2 tsp freshly ground black pepper (10mL)

Directions:

- Combine ingredients in a stainless steel bowl and whisk until sugar and salt are dissolved.

- Taste for seasoning, adding sugar or salt as necessary. The sauce should be hot but not sour.

Serves 4

TARRAGON MAYONNAISE

1 cup white wine (250mL)

3 sprigs of fresh tarragon

1 cup mayonnaise (250mL)

2 drops of Tabasco, or to taste

Directions:

- In a saucepan combine white wine and tarragon sprig. On medium heat reduce to 1/4 cup. Strain and chill.

- Mix the chilled reduction with mayonnaise and add 2 splashes of Tabasco sauce. Refrigerate until time to serve.

Yields 2 cups

TOMATO BBQ SAUCE

1/2 cup ketchup (125mL)

1/2 cup sugar (125mL)

3/4 can crushed tomatoes (175mL)

1 tbsp paprika (15mL)

1 tbsp dry mustard (15mL)

1 tsp cayenne pepper (5mL)

5 cloves garlic, chopped

1/2 onion, chopped

Directions:

- Add ingredients to a pot and simmer over low heat for 20 minutes.

- Refrigerate mixture overnight before serving.

Yields 2 cups

Market location photography:

Taryn Manias, *McArthur & Company*
Linda Pellowe and David Szolcsanyi, *Mad Dog Design Connection*

5/07-#
10/07 W